Frontier Military Series
IV

Military Governments in California

1846-1850

with a chapter on their prior use in
Louisiana, Florida and New Mexico

by

THEODORE GRIVAS

Associate Professor of History
Sonoma State College

The Arthur H. Clark Company
Glendale, California
1963

COPYRIGHT © 1963, BY
THE ARTHUR H. CLARK COMPANY

LIBRARY OF CONGRESS CATALOG CARD NUMBER 62-7925

Contents

Illustrations

Preface

Although the American occupation of California is a topic familiar to students of California history, for it encompasses such well-known events as the gold rush and the establishment of the State constitution and government, little has been done, heretofore, to investigate the many ramifications of the occupation government. Aside from a few incidental treatments of California's military governments done only as parts of works of much broader scope, no comprehensive study of military rule in California per se has been undertaken. Indeed California and Western United States historians touch upon a few phases of this topic in their treatment of the history of California. Unfortunately, many misconceptions appear regarding the true nature of the occupation government, some historians considering it military, and others civil.

One serious task of the author has been to establish clearly the true nature of the occupation government existing in California between July 7, 1846 and December 20, 1849. Despite pronouncements of civil government by American military governors in California, military rule prevailed throughout this entire period. Military officers were appointed governors by the executive branch of the federal government and relied on armed forces for their support. Congress, on the other hand, which has the constitutional right to provide civil government for the territories, did not act.

During the entire period of the military occupation of California the governors, who came from both naval and army ranks, relied for their support mainly on the troops that they commanded. Several of these governors fancied themselves civil governors. This, however, was not the case, for the military was always dominant over the civil authority. Furthermore, Congress had failed to provide a civil government after the Treaty of Guadalupe Hidalgo had been signed. Actually, when civil government finally came to California it was principally through the efforts of the citizens themselves, with the support and best wishes of the military government. As soon as the state constitution was established and the state government put in operation with elected officials, the military government turned over complete control to the civil authorities. Although Congress did not officially approve this civil government for almost a year, the military ceased to rule in California as of December 20, 1849.

In developing this study the author found it advisable to adopt a topical approach. There is, therefore, some overlapping in the various chapters, but this, the author believes, is necessary both for emphasis and continuity within each individual chapter. Great care, however, has been taken to reduce any "retelling" to the barest possible minimum.

Research for this study has not taken the author out of the state of California, primarily due to the availability of microfilmed documents from the National Archives. One of the main sources for documents has been the Bancroft Library at the University of California at Berkeley, where many valuable manuscript collections pertaining to the period of American occupation of California are available. The California State Library at Sacramento furnished its very important copies of early California newspapers. In San Marino, the Huntington Library provided manuscript materials and rare books. The Special Collections Library at the University of California at Los Angeles, the Los Angeles Public Library, the Los Angeles County Library, and the Doheny Library at the University of Southern California, have also been sources of significant material. The author wishes to express his gratitude to staff members of these various libraries, and to Dr. Donald C. Cutter and others of the department of history at the University of Southern California for their many courtesies.

To the John Randolph and Dora B. Haynes Foundation for its generous research grant, which resulted in the early completion of this study, the author remains forever indebted. Heartfelt gratitude is particularly extended to the author's wife, Jacqueline Smith Grivas for her cheerful encouragment and indispensable assistance rendered in numerous ways.

THEODORE GRIVAS

September 1961

United States Military Governments Prior to 1850

An inquiry into a specific administration of United States military government necessarily requires, for purposes of background and introduction, an examination of the various forms of military rule. Although the major emphasis of this study is military government in California between 1846 and 1850, a knowledge of previous experiments with military government in United States history is almost imperative in order to trace meaningfully the development of military rule prior to its application in California.

Basically, in the United States, there are three forms of military control – military law, martial law, and military government.[1] Military law is the legal code supporting the governmental structure of the military and naval forces. Applicable only to military personnel, military law is embodied in the "Uniform Code of Military Justice." [2] Within

---

[1] *Ex parte Milligan,* 4 Wallace, 141. In rendering the dissenting opinion Chief Justice Salmon P. Chase entered into a discussion of military jurisprudence in which he vaguely defined three forms of military government; see also William E. Birkhimer, *Military Government and Martial Law,* pp. 1-10.

[2] This was formerly divided into the "Articles of War" for the army and the "Articles for the Government of the Navy" for the navy. Since May 5, 1950, however, military law for all services is the "Uniform Code of Military Justice," Public Law 506, 81 Cong., sec. 64, statute 108.

the framework of military law there exists a series of tribunals with rather precise jurisdiction. Although these courts permit civilian lawyers to represent defendants, military law itself applies only to armed forces personnel.[3]

A second form of military control, martial law, is perhaps the best known and the most arbitrary. Instituted by the president of the United States or the governor of a state, martial law is proclaimed in areas where disaster or enemy invasion has made the local governmental forces ineffective.[4] Although temporary in nature, martial law, when proclaimed, overrides and supersedes all civil law. Moreover, the senior military officer in the area becomes the supreme authority, governing by fiat.[5] During a period of martial law, certain aspects of the existing civil code may be retained and enforced, according to the will of the military commander. In all cases the normal order is reversed, for the military power is supreme, while the civil is subordinate. Martial law is rarely lasting; therefore, even in extreme circumstances, civil laws are never repealed or annulled but merely temporarily suspended. At the time of its application, however, martial law apparently has no limits concerning its

[3] George B. Davis, *A Treatise on the Military Law of the United States,* p. 107.

[4] U.S. Const. Art. I, sec. 9, cl. 2. "The Privilege of the Writ of Habeas Corpus shall not be suspended, unless when in Cases of Rebellion or Invasion of the Public Safety may require it." The guarantee of the federal government to protect the states against foreign invasion is stated in the *U.S. Const., Art.* IV, sec. 4.

[5] Davis, *op. cit.,* p. 306.

authority.[6] In reality it is no law at all, and may be better expressed as martial rule. A specialist on the subject of martial law defines it as being:

> . . . the suspension of all law but the will of the commanders entrusted with its execution, to be exercised according to their judgment, the exigencies of the moment, and the usages of the service with no fixed and settled rules and laws, no definite practice, and not bound even by the rules of the military law.[7]

A third form of military control is military government. This, again, is a form of arbitrary government with few if any codified laws. Limited only by international law,[8] military government derives its authority from the customs of war and not the municipal law.[9] In its extreme form, military government is omnipotent. The military commander can, therefore, take almost any measures if the situation be deemed an emergency. Because of its wide jurisdiction, military government differs only slightly from martial law. For purposes of this study, therefore, the only distinction to be noted is that military government is proclaimed solely in enemy or recently acquired territory. Although some authorities have patiently and copiously differentiated between martial law and military

---

[6] Charles Fairman, *The Law of Martial Rule*, p. 20.

[7] Davis, *op. cit.*, p. 307.

[8] The senior military officer in command of a district under military government may have certain limits placed on his authority by Congress. This is rarely done. More recently international conferences have issued some limitations to military government, but a military commander can still take almost any course under urgent necessity.

[9] H. W. Halleck, *International Law*, pp. 776-77.

government, it appears that the characteristics of one are but different manifestations of the other.[10] Simply stated, therefore, military government is an extension of martial law into enemy territory.[11]

Authorization for martial law and/or military government in the United States is derived from the Constitution which (1) provides for the maintenance of a militia,[12] (2) authorizes its use "to execute laws of the Union, suppress insurrections, and repel invasions," [13] and (3) grants the president wide powers during war as "commander in chief of the army and navy of the United States, and of the militia of the several states." [14] The terms "martial law" and "military government" are neither listed nor defined in the Constitution; yet both are proclaimed by the President by virtue of his powers as commander in chief.

In terms of objectives another distinction between the two forms of government should be observed. Martial law supports civil government; military government supplants it. When there is a threat to the public safety, martial law is proclaimed primarily to buttress the failing civil authorities. Military government, on the other hand, is proclaimed in occupied enemy or newly acquired territory to supplant the existing government until the treaty of peace has been signed or until Congress has organized the area as a territory of the United States.[15] No constitutional limits are

---

10 Birkhimer, *op. cit.*, p. 179.

11 *Ibid.*, p. 1.

12 *U.S. Const.*, Art. I, sec. 7, cl. 15.

13 *Ibid.*, cl. 16.

14 *Ibid.*, Art. II, sec. 2, cl. 1.

15 Davis, *op. cit.*, pp. 107-9.

placed upon these two forms of government, but, in the opinion of many jurists, due moderation and justice should be exercised by the military commander.[16] In cases of abuse under both martial law and military government proper redress has been obtained in civil courts once civil authority has been restored. Recognizing this, Congress has in many cases passed acts of indemnity protecting military officers from prosecution for acts performed while administering military rule.[17]

The course of military government in the United States has necessarily followed its course of expansion. Striking a middle ground between the colonial theory of Ancient Greece, whose colonies acquired independence at the expense of the mother states, and Rome, whose colonies bore the expense of the mother country's expansion, the United States had been faced with the problem of military government only four times up to the period of 1850.

Rapid settlement of the trans-Appalachian west increased the importance of the control of the mouth of the Mississippi River – a river that was the major highway for the transportation of western settlers' products. The Treaty of San Lorenzo with Spain in 1796 guaranteed for a limited time the free navigation of the Mississippi River and the right of deposit of United States goods at New Orleans.[18] By the turn of the century, however, it

---

[16] James Lorimer, *The Institutes of the Law of Nations,* p. 343.

[17] *Bean* v. *Beckwith,* 18 Wallace, 510.

[18] William M. Malloy, *Treaties, Conventions, International Acts and Agreements,* 61 Cong., 2 sess., pp. 508-16.

became increasingly clear that the right of deposit would soon be revoked. As a result of a secret treaty concluded in 1800, Spain agreed to retrocede the Louisiana Territory to France, and Napoleon's carefully laid plans to re-establish the French Colonial Empire in America seemed almost fulfilled. Three years later, however, Napoleon, having suffered diplomatic and military reverses, startled the American emissary, Robert Livingston, by offering to sell the entire area of Louisiana, despite the fact that it was not yet in the possession of France.[19] For a consideration of fifteen million dollars and the cancellation of two million dollars of United States claims against the French government, the territory was ceded to the United States, when the treaty of cession was proclaimed on October 21, 1803.[20]

Among the articles of the treaty two are of particular note, since their constitutionality was successfully challenged at a later period.[21] Article

---

[19] Message of the President of the U.S., Oct. 17, 1803, *Debates and Proceedings of the Congress of the United States,* 8 Cong., 1 sess., pp. 18*ff.*

[20] Malloy, *op. cit.,* pp. 508-16.

[21] *American State Papers, Documents Legislative and Executive of the Congress of the United States,* Class 1 Foreign Relations, v, pp. 650-52. Article 3 was not fulfilled until Louisiana came into the Union as a state. Constitutionally, annexation does not mean that the inhabitants of a newly acquired territory become citizens immediately. Congress must specifically extend these Constitutional privileges to the newly acquired area. *Downes* v. *Bidwell,* 182 U.S. 244. Article 7 was also inconsistent with Constitutional provision. Secretary of State John Q. Adams explained to the French ambassador in 1821 that after the admission of Louisiana as a state, continued observance of favoritism to French and Spanish ships in its ports was an open viola-

three stated that the inhabitants of the ceded territory would be immediately incorporated within
the union with the usual advantages and privileges
accorded to citizens of the United States. In the
meantime the inhabitants were to be granted the
basic rights of life, liberty, and freedom of
worship. Article seven granted special privileges
to Spain and France for a period of twelve years
in the ports of Louisiana. Thereafter France was
to be "treated upon the footing of the most favored
nations in the ports of Louisiana." [22]

President Thomas Jefferson successfully justified
the purchase of Louisiana within his strong con-
structionalist views and prepared for the occupation of the territory. He asked Congress for a bill
to provide for immediate occupation and for
authority to establish a temporary military government. Granted power, Jefferson ordered the military to occupy the area and protect United States
interests.[23] Extraordinary powers, embracing all
phases of government, were to be vested in a military governor appointed by the president. William
Charles Cole Claiborne, then governor of Mississippi Territory, and General James Wilkinson
were authorized by the President to take possession
of the Louisiana Territory, and it was accomplished peacefully on December 20, 1803, in the

tion of the Constitution which required that all duties, imposts and
excises be uniform throughout all the states.

[22] Malloy, *op. cit.*, pp. 508-16.

[23] W. C. C. Claiborne, New Orleans, to James Madison, Washington, Dec. 20, 1803, *Debates and Proceedings,* 8 Cong., 1 sess., p. 1231.

solemn presence of the inhabitants of New Orleans.[24] The commissioners later translated the solemnity of the occasion as "amidst the reiterated acclamation of thousands."[25]

For the most part the inhabitants of Louisiana were from the very beginning rather dubious of the rewards to be gained by United States citizenship. Despite the enigmatic remarks of Governor Claiborne who proclaimed that "the inhabitants thereof will be incorporated in the union of the United States and admitted as soon as possible according to the principles of the Federal Constitution,"[26] the Louisianians remained unimpressed.[27] Probably more to their liking was the section of the proclamation which promised them liberty, property and the pursuit of their religion, and also the statement:

> . . . that all laws and municipal regulations which were in existence at the cessation of the late government remain in full force; and that all civil officers charged with their execution . . . are continued in their function during the pleasure of the governor. . .[28]

The white inhabitants of the area who were chiefly descendant from French and Canadian stock and, therefore, had an almost congenital dis-

---

[24] *Ibid.*

[25] James Alexander Robertson, *Louisiana Under the Rule of Spain, France and the United States,* II, p. 225.

[26] Proclamation, W. C. C. Claiborne, Dec. 20, 1803, *Debates and Proceedings,* 8 Cong., 1 sess., p. 1231.

[27] Charles Gayarre, *History of Louisiana: The American Domination,* I, pp. 1-2.

[28] Proclamation, W. C. C. Claiborne, *op. cit.,* pp. 1231-32.

trust for the Anglo-American, glumly awaited the worst.[29] During the life of military government in Louisiana, Governor Claiborne was vested with the same powers as the former Governor-General and the Intendant of Louisiana, thereby making him the undisputed autocrat of the area.[30]

One of Claiborne's first measures was the establishment of the Court of Pleas on October 30, 1803, which was composed of seven justices all appointed by him. Civil jurisdiction of this court was limited to cases not exceeding three thousand dollars in value. Right of appeal to the governor, however, was granted. Criminal cases of a minor sort came under the jurisdiction of this court. Sitting as individuals, the seven justices had summary jurisdiction in cases involving sums under one hundred dollars – the right of appeal in these cases going to the Court of Pleas, that is, the seven justices sitting as a body.[31]

In order to meet the demand for a circulating medium Governor Claiborne established the Louisiana Bank, an institution entirely unknown to the people. Although financial stringency was somewhat relieved by this institution, the fears of the people were greatly aroused as they associated the bank script with the *assignats* and *liberanzas*.[32] Efforts were also bent at this time by Claiborne

---

[29] Gayarre, *op. cit.*, I, p. 1.   [30] *Ibid.*, p. 2.

[31] Francois Xavier Martin, *The History of Louisiana*, p. 241.

[32] Gayarre, *op. cit.*, I, p. 15. *Assignats* were government notes and bonds which eventually became worthless. *Liberanzas* were Spanish counterparts.

toward organizing a militia, but the incorporation of Americans within the native militia resulted in distrust and its eventual dissolution.[33]

Regarding the smaller administrative units, Claiborne commissioned Dr. John Watkins to visit the parishes and villages and inform the people of the change in government. Watkins had migrated to Louisiana from Kentucky and had married a French Louisiana girl. His knowledge of the language and his excellent reputation among the French Canadians made Watkins a valuable agent for the United States.[34] In his travels to the various parishes and villages, Watkins was charged with responsibility to retain as many of the former officers as he could, and, if they declined, he was to nominate successors.[35]

More displeasure with the military government of Louisiana resulted by the United States' refusal to extend its revenue laws to Louisiana until February 24, 1804. For a period of almost five months, therefore, the United States enforced the Spanish customs laws in Louisiana, an utter disregard of a constitutional provision, since the Constitution specifies that "all Duties, Imposts and Excises shall be uniform throughout the United States." [36] By enforcing the Spanish customs laws the Jefferson administration violated a constitutional principle.

---

[33] *Ibid.*, pp. 4-6.   [34] Robertson, *op. cit.*, II, p. 310.

[35] *Ibid.*, pp. 309-10; Dunbar Rowland, ed., *Official Letter Books of W. C. C. Claiborne, 1801-1816,* pp. 367-68.

[36] *U.S. Const.*, Art. I, sec. 8, cl. I.

The treaty with France made no reference to customs laws, and, therefore, once the treaty was mutually ratified the *political* laws of the United States immediately and automatically superseded the Spanish. Though only implied in the treaty, this principle was affirmed by the Supreme Court in 1828. The majority opinion stated that:

> The same act which transfers their country transfers the allegiance of those who remain in it; and the law which may be denominated political is necessarily changed, although that which regulates the intercourse and general conduct of individuals remains in force, until altered by the newly created power of the state.[37]

The hated six per cent tax of the Spanish that was collected by American officials, did not increase the popularity of the Americans in Louisiana.[38]

In March, 1804, an act was passed and approved by the President dividing the area of Louisiana and creating a Territory of the southern portion of it.[39] This act, however, was not to take effect until the following October. The period of military government in Louisiana, therefore, was almost a year, for contrary to some authorities, the period between the passage of the organic act and its declared effectiveness must be considered as a continuation of military government.[40]

---

[37] *American Insurance Company* v. *Cantor* (1828). 1 Peters, 511.

[38] Robertson, *op. cit.,* I, p. 179.

[39] Government of Louisiana, Mar. 17, 1804, *Debates and Proceedings,* 8 Cong., 1 sess., pp. 1198 ff.

[40] Remonstrance of the People of Louisiana, Dec. 31, 1804, *Debates and Proceedings,* 8 Cong., 2 sess., p. 1598.

Opposition to the military government mounted, and finally, when it became organized, a petition was sent both to the congress and to the president listing grievances.[41] The petitions stated generally that the inhabitants of Louisiana were dissatisfied with the United States' occupation for several reasons: (1) the governor was an utter stranger to their laws, customs, traditions, and language, (2) the government had no personal interest in the prosperity of the land, (3) the governor was surrounded with Anglo-Americans to whom he gave decided preference in office holding, (4) the Court of Pleas was composed of judges of Anglo-American descent who were ignorant of the laws and of the language, proceedings being carried out in English, a language most of the Louisianians did not understand, and (5) the mistakes made by the government in Louisiana went without redress because the highest appeal was to the governor of the province. Adding to the displeasure of Louisianans was the act passed to separate the province into Upper and Lower Louisiana. This, they felt, was calculated to divide them and, therefore, diminish the importance of the province.[42]

By October, 1804, southern Louisiana had passed to the status of a territory, and the northern portion was placed under the jurisdiction of the governor of the Indiana Territory.[43] The inhabitants of the

[41] *Ibid.*

[42] *Ibid.*, pp. 1598-1607.

[43] Petition of the People of Louisiana, Jan. 4, 1805, *American State Papers,* I, Misc., p. 403.

northern portion of Louisiana, especially in the
principal city of St. Louis, deemed this despotic
bondage and chose delegates to a convention to
protest it. From the five major settlements, including St. Louis, sixteen members penned their grievances and appointed two delegates, Augustus
Chouteau and Elijas Fromentin, to take the petition to the Congress of the United States.[44] By
March 3, 1805, however, an act was passed creating
a first grade of territorial government, and,
although a military man occupied a civilian office
this cannot be considered as a military government.[45]

Complaints of abuses suffered by the inhabitants
of Louisiana were never directed toward the military governor, William C. C. Claiborne. It was
recognized that he was merely representing the
United States government. The enmity of the
Louisianans was reserved for the federal government, whose philosophy of democracy seemingly
was inapplicable to the territory of Louisiana during the period of military government.[46] Claiborne, on the other hand, was highly respected and
continued as governor of the Territory and was
first governor under the state constitution, ultimately serving in the United States Senate.[47]

---

[44] *Ibid.*

[45] An Act Providing for the government of the District of Louisiana,
Mar. 3, 1805, *Debates and Proceedings,* 8 Cong., 2 sess., pp. 1684-85.

[46] Gayarre, *op. cit.,* p. 2.

[47] *Ibid.,* p. 2, *passim.* William Charles Cole Claiborne was born in
Virginia in 1775. Educated as a lawyer, he was appointed Governor
of the Mississippi Territory at the age of twenty-six. Two years later

Despite the local opposition to it, the first United States experiment in military government proved successful in terms of objectives, for the interests of the government were protected without any display of violence, and the area was eventually incorporated into the family of states.

Annexation of the Florida area by the United States brought with it another term of military government. Having been divided by the Spanish into West and East Florida, the area was systematically swallowed up by the United States in the second decade of the eighteenth century. Jefferson had early supported the view that the Louisiana Territory included the area of West Florida from the Mississippi River on the west to the Perdido River on the east. When successful American filibusters proclaimed the independent state of the Republic of West Florida,[48] in 1810, the United States decided to act. Accordingly on October 27 of that year, President Madison issued a proclamation declaring the United States' possession of the area of West Florida to the Perdido River.

Adding it to the governmental jurisdiction of the Territory of Orleans, Madison ordered Governor Claiborne to occupy West Florida and

---

he was chosen as the military governor of Louisiana. Although respected and admired by the Louisianians, Claiborne secretly questioned their ability to adjust to a democratic form of government. In a letter to President Madison on January 2, 1804, he stated: "I could wish that the Constitution to be given to this district may be as republican as the people can be safely entrusted with. But the principles of a popular government are illy suited to the present state of Society in this Province." Robertson, *Louisiana,* II, p. 233.

[48] Hubert Bruce Fuller, *The Purchase of Florida,* p. 282-90.

defend the United States' interests.[49] By the outbreak of the War of 1812, the area of West Florida
was securely in the hands of the United States,
much to the chagrin of filibusters who had
proclaimed the republic.[50] The Mobile District
including the seaport city of Mobile came into the
possession of the United States after the War of
1812. West Florida continued in a quasi territory-
military state until its eventual partition into the
states of Louisiana, Mississippi and Alabama.[51]

Annexation of the territory of West Florida only
whetted the United States' appetite for more of the
Spanish colony, and soon East Florida bristled
with intrigue. By 1818, East Florida had become a
fortified haven for renegade Indians and runaway
slaves whose attacks on Georgia border settlements
brought immediate retaliation from the United
States.[52] Crossing the Spanish Florida border,
American troops under the command of General
Andrew Jackson extended their "punitive expedition" to one of conquest and on April 7, 1818,
seized the city of St. Marks.[53] By May 24, Amer-

---

[49] Caroline Mays Brevard, *A History of Florida*, p. 28-29.

[50] *Ibid.*, p. 25 *ff.* Claiborne's observations on the possible acquisition
of West Florida were made clear to President Madison early in 1814.
He wrote: "I believe myself that Spain is jealous of our pretentions to
the west, and that it would be no difficult task to obtain a cession of
both Floridas for a relinquishment of our claims to all the country
west to the Sabine River. I believe also, that if we were to insist upon
our claim (under the Treaty of Cession) to the Country as far as
Perdigo [sic], Spain would be disposed to concede, unless indeed she
should be encouraged in a refusal by France. . ." Robertson,
Louisiana, II, p. 237.

[51] Fuller, *op. cit.*, p. 199.

[52] *Ibid.*, pp. 238-40.   [53] *Ibid.*

ican troops were in Pensacola, and two days later articles of capitulation were signed. That Jackson exceeded his authority cannot be denied, for United States troops occupied an area belonging to a foreign power while both countries were at peace. Furthermore his orders from Secretary of War, John C. Calhoun, were to pursue the renegades to the border and then await further orders. No further orders were given him.

During the occupation Alexander Arbuthnot and Robert Ambrister, two British traders in Florida, suspected of inciting the Indians and Negroes to attack American settlements, were arrested and courtmartialed by Jackson and subsequently executed.[54] Although severely criticized for this action in the United States and England, Jackson has been vindicated by some authorities who claim he was progressing under the aegis of international law. They claim that the authority for this "special court" which condemned the British traders was vested in the laws of war, and that these people had violated them. There was, however, no war.[55]

From April 7, 1818, to February 8, 1819, American troops held the territory of St. Marks and Pensacola. Jackson, declaring Spain incapable of controlling marauding Indians, appointed a military and civil governor. No military man held any other office and civil officers were appointed from among the citizens. Spanish law and custom were retained for the most part. On February 8, 1819,

---

[54] Birkhimer, *op. cit.*, pp. 277-78.   [55] *Ibid.*

the United States returned this area to the Spanish.[56]

Earlier, on November 12, 1817, Amelia Island on the east coast of Florida was occupied by the United States Navy in order to break up a nest of pirates under the command of Luis Aury. Military government complete with customs laws was established and maintained until American acquisition of the entire area of Florida.[57]

Jackson's Florida campaign at first embarrassed the United States government. By 1819, however, the Florida raids were used to strengthen the American position in negotiations with Spain. Spain was accused of aiding and abetting hostilities against the Americans. In the resulting Adams-Onis Treaty of 1819 Spain renounced all claims to West Florida and ceded East Florida to the United States.[58] On the other hand, the United States assumed the claims of its own citizens against Spain to the maximum amount of five million dollars and also renounced all claims to the Texas area. Ratifications of the Adams-Onis Treaty were not exchanged until two years after its signing. On March 3, 1821, Congress passed an act authorizing the president to take possession of the area of East Florida and to appoint the necessary people to administer the military government.[59] Essentially, the military governor of the Florida area was granted the same powers and authority as had been

---

[56] Brevard, *op. cit.*, p. 57 *ff.*   [57] *Ibid.*, pp. 47-48.

[58] Fuller, *op. cit.*, pp. 298-300.

[59] Sidney Walter Martin, *Florida During the Territorial Days*, pp. 15-19.

granted to the governor of Louisiana in 1803. A provision in the same act, however, stated that the revenue laws of the United States were extended to Florida and the President was authorized to appoint necessary people to administer the customs laws.

The military governorship fell to the controversial Andrew Jackson. This served to vindicate his highhanded action in the Floridas a few years before. Doubtless, however, President Monroe also considered the importance of a strong governor in the Floridas when he made his appointment of Jackson. He knew Jackson to be both respected and feared by the Spaniards.[60]

Under Spanish administration, Florida had been divided into two separate administrative districts, East Florida and West Florida, with a governor at Pensacola and one at St. Augustine. In planning his administration of the Floridas, Jackson provided for a secretary for each of the provinces hoping to make the appointments himself. He was, however, overruled in this regard by President Monroe who appointed the secretary for East Florida, William G. D. Worthington. On July 10, 1821, East Florida was formally delivered into the hands of the United States and a week later, on July 17, Jackson formally accepted West Florida as United States territory.[61]

Jackson immediately plunged into the work of governmentally organizing the two areas. He investigated the position of alcalde and appointed

---

[60] *Ibid.*, p. 16.   [61] *Ibid.*, p. 18.

Henry M. Brackenridge to the post. Provision was also made for all Spanish citizens wishing to become American citizens to register. At the end of a twelve month period if their names were still on the roll books, Jackson agreed to consider them citizens. This "citizen making" provision, however, was rescinded by Congress who deemed this a power vested only in them. As a result of Mrs. Jackson's puritanical sensibilities the governor also put through an ordinance which closed the theaters and gambling houses on Sunday. Then turning to the judiciary, Jackson established a series of county courts and provided for jury trials.[62]

The military governorship of Florida, however, frustrated Jackson more and more, primarily because of President Monroe's independent appointments of subordinate officers in the Florida government. Jackson, as always, wanted to be dominant in command and to place men he considered competent in the important jobs. Administration policy in Washington, however, determined that Jackson's power should be curbed.[63] At length Jackson, wearied of the job and the constant opposition, tendered his resignation to President Monroe saying:

> I can only observe for the present and I am wearied of public life, I want rest and my private concern imperiously demand my attention. [*sic*] [64]

---

[62] Brevard, *op. cit.*, pp. 65-66; Martin, *op. cit.*, p. 31.

[63] John S. Bassett, *The Life of Andrew Jackson*, p. 317; Marquis James, *The Life of Andrew Jackson*, p. 327.

[64] J. S. Bassett, ed., *Jackson Correspondence*, III, p. 143.

Accepting the letter of resignation on December 21, 1821, President Monroe expressed his gratitude for and appreciation of Jackson's admirable record in Florida. The two secretaries, Worthington and George Walton were continued in their governmental posts in East and West Florida until March 30, 1822, when Congress passed the organic law providing for the three branches of government: executive, legislative and judicial departments in Florida. Territorial status was thus proclaimed in Florida, after a rather stormy siege of military government.[65]

The area of the great southwest, including primarily New Mexico and California, came under United States military government as a result of the Mexican War in 1846. Brigadier General Stephen Watts Kearny in command of the Army of the West left Fort Leavenworth with some two thousand men on June 5, 1846, bound for Santa Fe. Following the Santa Fe trail, the Army of the West entered the city of Santa Fe unopposed on August 18, 1846.[66] Basically the orders stressed the fact that Kearny was to assure the Mexican people that the objectives of the United States in occupying the territory were to "liberate them from tyrants and to provide for them a free government, with the least possible delay" [67] similar to that of

[65] Brevard, *op. cit.,* p. 71.

[66] Theodore Grivas, "General Stephen Watts Kearny and the Army of the West," p. 10.

[67] W. L. Marcy, Washington, to S. W. Kearny, Fort Leavenworth, June 3, 1846, *U.S. Gov. Doc. Ser. 499,* p. 6.

WILLIAM C. C. CLAIBORNE
Appointed in 1804 as military governor of Lower Louisiana
Territory, and later was elected governor and senator from
the State of Louisiana. From Fortier's *History of Louisiana.*

the existing United States territories. In the implimentation of the "free government" Kearny was to call upon the people "to exercise the rights of freemen in selecting their own representatives to the territorial legislature." [68] A conciliatory attitude was to be taken, and Kearny was ordered to establish civil government and abolish any existing arbitrary provisions of law. The orders also encouraged the continuance in office of any Mexican officials who would take the oath of allegiance to the United States. [69]

A proclamation was, therefore, issued by Kearny on August 22 to the effect that a representative government would soon be established in New Mexico. [70] By September 22 Kearny had proclaimed a civil government, and appointed a full list of civil officers. These included a governor, a secretary of state, three justices of a supreme court, a United States attorney and marshal, a prefect, an auditor, treasurer, attorney general, and two district attorneys. Steps were also taken to make New Mexico a territory of the United States. The Missouri Organic Law as provided by Congress was adopted as the organic law of the territory. An election for a delegate to Congress and for members of a General Assembly was planned for August 1847. [71]

A notable and lasting achievement of this new government was a compilation of laws known as

[68] *Ibid.*   [69] *Ibid.*
[70] *Ibid.,* Proclamation, Kearny, Aug. 22, 1846, pp. 20-21.
[71] *1897: Compiled Laws of New Mexico,* pp. 65-90.

the Kearny Code.[72] This contained a code of laws consisting of forty-two pages which were assembled by Colonel A. W. Doniphan with the assistance of a private, W. P. Hall, who had been recently elected congressman from the state of Missouri.[73] These laws were compiled from Mexican laws, modified to conform to the constitution of the United States, and laws of the states of Missouri and Texas.[74] Devoting nearly three pages to revenue regulations, the Kearny Code also defined crimes, fixed punishment, provided for the administration of justice, with trial by jury, and introduced *habeas corpus.*[75]

In the organization of civil government in New Mexico General Kearny performed commendable service, but he either misinterpreted his orders or deliberately exceeded them. By proclaiming New Mexico a territory of the United States, he had preceded the Treaty of Guadalupe Hidalgo by over two years.[76] Actually the province was only *occupied* by the United States, and, despite the eagerness of the Americans to annex this territory formally, the only legal means of annexation re-

---

[72] James M. Cutts, *The Conquest of California and New Mexico,* pp. 64-5.

[73] Kearny, Santa Fe, to the Adjutant General, Washington, Sept. 22, 1846, *U.S. Gov. Doc. Ser. 499,* p. 26. Concerning the code, Kearny stated, "I take great pleasure in stating that I am entirely indebted for these laws to Colonel A. W. Doniphan, of the 1st regiment of Missouri mounted volunteers, who received much assistance from private Willard Hall of his regiment."

[74] *Compiled Laws,* pp. 65-66.   [75] *Ibid.*

[76] Treaty of Guadalupe Hidalgo, *U.S. Gov. Doc. Ser. 5646,* p. 1107.

mained in a treaty with Mexico.[77] General Winfield Scott made this point when he sent further instructions to Kearny regarding operations in California. He said:

> You will not, however, declare the province to be annexed. Permanent incorporation of a territory must depend on the government of the United States.[78]

As chief executive of this so-called civil government General Kearny appointed Charles Bent, a native of Virginia, who had been in the New Mexico area since 1832. For other posts, Kearny wisely chose native men including Anciana Vigal, as secretary, and Antonio José Otero, as a member of the Supreme Court.[79] By September 16, Kearny, having visited many of the areas surrounding Santa Fe, was convinced that change of government had agreed with the New Mexicans. In a dispatch to Washington Kearny stated:

> The inhabitants of the country were found to be highly satisfied and contented and apparently vied with each other to see who could show us the greatest hospitality and kindness.[80]

Eager to comply with his orders, which were to continue to California when he deemed it safe to

---

[77] *U.S. Const.* Art. IV, sec. 3, cl. 1.

[78] Winfield Scott, Washington, to Kearny, Nov. 3, 1846, *U.S. Gov. Doc. Ser. 499,* p. 14.

[79] Kearny, Santa Fe, to Adjutant General, Washington, Sept. 22, 1846, *ibid.,* p. 26.

[80] Kearny, Santa Fe, to R. Jones, Washington, Sept. 16, 1846, *ibid.,* pp. 25-26.

leave New Mexico, Kearny with three hundred mounted dragoons left Santa Fe on September 26.[81] Hardly had Kearny and his dragoons disappeared over the horizon when plans were formulated by Indians in the vicinity of Santa Fe for one of their typical concerted attacks. The arrival of Colonel Sterling Price with a regiment of Missouri volunteers, on November 6, forced the Indians to delay their plans. Several days later an informer betrayed the Indians and the attack was quelled before it could begin.[82] A few weeks later, however, the angry Indians gained revenge by murdering several governmental officers including the governor, Charles Bent.[83] A period of martial law was then ordered by Colonel Price. A number of months went by as Indian conspirators were apprehended, trials held, and executions performed. The quasi-civil government was again restored with the appointment by Colonel Price of Secretary Vigal as governor on December 17, 1847.[84]

The Treaty of Guadalupe Hidalgo was proclaimed on May 30, 1848, and thereby the territory of New Mexico was legally annexed to the United States. But beginning with the administration of Governor Vigal, December 17, 1847 – March 3, 1851, when a Territorial government was declared,

---

[81] W. H. Emory, *U.S. Gov. Ser. 517*, pp. 45-46.

[82] Hubert H. Bancroft, *History of Arizona and New Mexico*, p. 420.

[83] Donanciano [sic] Vigal, Santa Fe, to James Buchanan, Washington, Feb. 16, 1847, *U.S. Gov. Doc. Ser. 521*, pp. 18-19.

[84] *Ibid.*

a period of disorder and confusion existed in New Mexico. Among the many complications occurring during this period were the boundary disputes with Texas, the inability to collect revenue, and the continued Indian depredations.[85] At one point two factions in New Mexico claimed to be in control of the government. One was the so-called "elected" government established under the Kearny Code; the other, Colonel J. M. Monroe, representing the United States government, who had assumed the title of military and civil governor.[86]

For almost five years, therefore, military government in New Mexico produced a period of disorder and confusion, thereby violating its original intent to protect life and property. Stability appeared with the Territorial government which had the tendency of uniting opposing factions to the one aim of representative government.[87]

In three applications of military government prior to the military government in California sufficient evidence is available to show that at best it was unwanted by the people – a people whose former government was almost as arbitrary as military rule. And yet from the standpoint of expediency and security military government served the United States well.

[85] Bancroft, *op. cit.,* pp. 426 ff.

[86] Ralph E. Twitchell, *The Leading Facts of New Mexican History,* pp. 265 ff.

[87] Bancroft, *op. cit.,* 426 ff.

Military Occupation of California

The premature occupation of California in 1842 by Commodore Thomas ap C. Jones had the effect of exposing United States' ambitions in California and on the Pacific coast.[1] Despite the apologies and acts of cordiality by the Americans, relations between the United States and Mexico continued steadily to grow worse, especially as the United States toyed with the Texas annexation questions. Complicating matters also was Mexico's refusal to pay its debt to the United States.[2] The prospect of war with Mexico seemed clear in some high official circles in Washington, for as early as 1845 precautionary measures were taken in the eventuality of the outbreak. Three dispatches were sent to Commodore John D. Sloat, commander of the Pacific squadron, by Secretary of the Navy George

[1] Believing rumors that war had been declared between the United States and Mexico and that a British fleet was on its way to occupy California, Commodore Jones made a swift voyage from Peru to Monterey arriving on Oct. 19, 1842. He forced the surrender of the city and raised the American flag. Two days later, convinced of his mistake, Commodore Jones ran down the United States flag and attempted to restore the *status quo*.

[2] Claims of American citizens resident in Mexico, who had suffered economic losses in damaged property as a result of periodic revolutions in Mexico, had been arbitrated by an international tribunal which awarded them about two million dollars against Mexico. Three installments were paid, when Mexico defaulted on the debt.

Bancroft in 1845. The earliest dispatch dated June 24, 1845 and labeled "secret and confidential" avowedly expressed the government's plan as regards California in the event of war. The Commodore was instructed to "ascertain with certainty that Mexico . . . [had] declared war against the United States," and then occupy "the port of San Francisco, and blockade or occupy such other ports" as his force would permit. In order to mollify any predatory implications in the letter a closing paragraph was added.[3]

> The great distance of your squadron, and the difficulty of communicating with you, are the causes for issuing this order. The President hopes most earnestly that the peace of the two countries may not be disturbed. The object of the instructions is to possess you of the views of the government in the event of a declaration of war against the United States – an event which you are enjoined to do everything consistent with the national honor on your part, to avoid.[4]

This paragraph however proved a source of anxiety and embarrassment to Commodore Sloat and caused him to delay the occupation of California for almost two months until he was certain that the United States and Mexico were at war.[5]

---

[3] George Bancroft, Washington, to John D. Sloat, June 24, 1845, *U.S. Gov. Doc. Ser. 520,* p. 231.

[4] *Ibid.*

[5] Some authorities have sharply criticized Commodore Sloat for his indecision despite "very specific orders" from Secretary Bancroft. The orders of June 24, as well as those of Aug. 5 and Oct. 17, 1845 are far from specific. Sloat possessed no further orders, and he doubtless remembered Commodore Jones' indiscretion of 1842 – factors that made

With the shedding of "American blood on American soil" war with Mexico was formally declared, and further instructions were sent to Sloat concerning the official policy in the occupation of California. On July 12, 1846 Secretary Bancroft dispatched the following instructions to Sloat:

> . . . the object of the United States under its rights as a belligerent nation, is to possess itself entirely of Upper California. . . The object of the United States has reference to ultimate peace with Mexico; and if, at that peace the basis of the *uti possidetis* shall be established, the government expects, through your forces, to be found in actual possession of California.[6]

The motives were thus clear, California was to be a war prize of the United States.

This very important dispatch, which unfortunately Sloat never received, instructed him, once in possession of California, to establish a "civil" administration under his protection. In the selection of persons to hold office due respect was to be shown "to the wishes of the people of California as well as to actual possessors of authority in that province." Sloat was further enjoined to allow as much self-government as was consistent with the

---

him overcautious. Rumors of war reached him as early as May 17, 1846, a letter to this effect being sent by William M. Wood, a discharged fleet surgeon returning home overland through Mexico. National Archives Microfilm 89, roll no. 32.

[6] Bancroft, Washington, to Sloat, July 12, 1846, *U.S. Gov. Doc. Ser. 520*, p. 238. *Uti possidetis* is a principle of international law which grants to belligerents as absolute property the area in possession of each at the time of the establishment of peace.

military occupation, and to assure the people that the United States forces were there for their protection. The confidential orders to Brigadier General Stephen Watts Kearny were also included with the dispatch informing Sloat of Kearny's march to California. The government, the dispatch concluded, expected "the land and naval forces to cooperate with each other in the most friendly and effective manner." [7]

Dispatches from Washington were usually three months en route to the Pacific coast; therefore Commodore Sloat had no official instruction after the outbreak of war with Mexico, but his occupation policy in California surprisingly anticipated the instructions from Washington which he never received. Sloat, perhaps indecisive, was, however, perceptive enough to realize a policy of conciliation, in a territory destined to become a part of the United States, was the only course to pursue.

On June 7, Commodore Sloat, having received more reliable reports of the outbreak of war, decided to act. Having earlier ordered several ships of his squadron to the California coast to await further instructions, he sailed for Monterey, arriving July 2.[8] The next five days he spent preparing his landing forces for the occupation of the capital of California. Orders were issued to his two hundred and fifty-man landing party stressing the importance of cultivating the good opinion of

[7] *Ibid.,* pp. 238-9.

[8] Sloat, Flag Ship "Levant," to Bancroft, July 31, 1846, N. A. Microfilm 89, roll no. 32.

the inhabitants, and adding that a conciliatory attitude was to be taken by all United States forces towards the Californians. On July 7, 1846, therefore, the troops under the command of Captain William Mervine landed and took possession of Monterey. At the nearby custom house the proclamation of Sloat was read to the inhabitants and the "standard of the United States hoisted amid three hearty cheers by the troops and foreigners present and a salute of twenty-one guns fired by all ships."

In the next several days the United States' flag was hoisted at San Francisco under the command of Captain John D. Montgomery and in Sonoma, Sacramento (Sutter's Fort), and San Jose. In each of these flag-raising ceremonies the proclamation of Sloat was furnished and read to the people. Sloat's proclamation began by declaring that the state of war existing between the United States and Mexico was caused by the latter because of its invasion of United States territory.[9] Sloat then continued:

> I declare to the inhabitants of California that, although I come in arms with a powerful force, I do not come among them as an enemy to California; on the contrary, I come as its best friend, and henceforth California will be a portion of the United States, and its peaceful inhabitants will enjoy the same rights and privileges as the citizens of any other portion of that territory, with all the rights and privileges they now enjoy, together with the privileges of

[9] Forces of General Marciano Arista crossed the Rio Grande River above Matamoros, Texas on April 24, 1846 and attacked American Forces. Eleven American dragoons of General Zachary Taylor's army were killed.

choosing their own magistrates and other officers for the administration of justice among themselves; and the same protection will be extended to them as to any other state in the Union. They will also enjoy permanent government, under which life, property, and the constitutional right and lawful security to worship the Creator in the way most congenial to one's sense of duty, will be secured, which unfortunately the central government of Mexico cannot afford them, destroyed as her resources are by internal factions and corrupt officers, who create constant revolutions to promote their own interests and impress the people.[10]

Under such conditions the country, Sloat predicted, will prosper and advance and, furthermore,

. . . the revenue laws will be the same in California as in all other parts of the United States, affording . . . [Californians] all manufactures and produce of the United States free from any duty, and all foreign goods at one quarter of the duty they now pay.[11]

The point was also emphasized that, as a result of United States' annexation, California's products and real estate would greatly increase in value to the benefit of the people of California. Sloat finally concluded, reassuring the Californians of his friendly intentions and stating that:

Such of the inhabitants of California, whether native or foreigners, as may not be disposed to accept the high privileges of citizenship and live peaceably under the government of the United States, will be allowed time to dispose of their property and to remove out of the country,

---

[10] Proclamation, Sloat, Monterey, July 7, 1846, *U.S. Gov. Doc. Ser. 493.* pp. 644-45.
[11] *Ibid.*

if they choose, without any restrictions; or remain in it, observing strict neutrality. With full confidence in the honor and integrity of the inhabitants of the country, I invite the judges, alcaldes, and other civil magistrates to retain their offices, and to execute their functions as heretofore, that the public tranquility may not be disturbed; at least, until the government of the territory can be more definitely arranged. All persons holding title to real estate, or in quiet possession of the lands under color of right, shall have these titles and rights guaranteed to them. All churches and property they contain in possession of the clergy of California shall continue in the same rights and possessions they now enjoy.

All provisions and supplies of every kind furnished by the inhabitants for the use of the United States ships and soldiers will be paid for at fair prices; and no private property will be taken for public use without just compensation at the moment.[12]

A more conciliatory attitude would have been hard to assume without losing some respect as a conqueror of the territory. And yet under the rules of war Commodore Sloat had wide powers as supreme commander in the area. It is the fundamental privilege of a belligerent to occupy and govern an area under its military control.[13] In Secretary of War William L. Marcy's instructions to General Stephen Watts Kearny of January 11, 1847, this point is clearly made.[14]

---

[12] *Ibid.,* p. 645. [13] See above, p. 15.

[14] Brigadier General Stephen Watts Kearny had been ordered immediately after the outbreak of war with Mexico to command the "Army of the West." Leading his 1st Dragoons and some 1700 Missouri Volunteers over the Santa Fe trail, Kearny entered the Mexican province of New Mexico and successfully occupied the city of Santa Fe. In faithful compliance to orders, he established a "civil"

Under the law of nations, the power conquering a territory or country has the right to establish a civil government
within the same, as a means of securing the conquest, and
with a view to protecting the persons and property of the
people, and it is not intended to limit you in the full
exercise of this authority. Indeed, it is desired you should
exercise it in such a manner as to inspire confidence in the
people that our power is to be firmly sustained in that
country.[15]

Some twenty-one days before Sloat's arrival a
group of insurgents, composed of United States
immigrants to California, had raised their own flag
at Sonoma, declaring an independent California
republic. Captain John C. Fremont of the United
States Army Topographical Engineers, who had
been in California on a "scientific survey" soon
assumed ex-officio command of the military forces
of the insurgents. But the appearance of the commodore at Monterey on the seventh of July
quashed all hopes of establishing a California
republic.[16]

After the flag was raised at Monterey on July 7,
Sloat communicated with the military commandant, Don Jose Castro, urging him to surrender his
troops and meet in conference with the commodore
at Monterey.[17] Two replies were sent by Castro to

---

government, and then proceeded with his dragoons to California.
Theodore Grivas, "General Stephen Watts Kearny and the Army of
the West," p. 2.

[15] Marcy, Washington, to Kearny, Jan. 11, 1847, *U.S. Gov. Doc. Ser.
573,* p. 244.

[16] For a full discussion of the "Bear Flag Revolt" see Hubert H.
Bancroft, *History of California,* vol. v.

Sloat, the first vituperatively condemning John C. Fremont and his barbarous band of followers.[18] The second letter stated that, as far as Castro was concerned, he would never surrender, and that in any case the governor and the assembly would have to be consulted in the formal capitulation of the province.[19] An invitation was then extended to Governor Pio Pico to join with Sloat in a conference at Monterey. Assurance was also given the governor and the people by Sloat, that he would prevent any further loss of life by curbing the activities of the insurgents to the north.[20]

Arrangements were also made by Sloat to meet with Brevet Captain John C. Fremont, a man who had assumed an enormous amount of authority in California. As commander of the party of one hundred and sixty mounted men, Fremont had imprisoned California military officials and conducted movements that resulted in the death of a number of men, had seized and appropriated private property and, in a word, waged a war against the Department of California. One would assume, as Sloat did, that Fremont possessed very special powers and detailed instructions from the government at Washington.

It was necessary, Sloat felt, that in the event of

[17] Sloat, Monterey, to Don Jose Castro, July 7, 1847, N. A. Microfilm 89, roll no. 32.

[18] Jose Castro, San Juan Bautista, to Señor Commander in Chief, July 9, 1846, *U.S. Gov. Doc. Ser. 499*, pp. 104-05.

[19] *Ibid.*

[20] Sloat, Monterey, to Don Pio Pico, Angeles, [sic], July 12, 1846, *U.S. Gov. Doc. Ser. 493*, pp. 649-50.

Castro's capitulation that Fremont's orders be known, and that he be present. On the nineteenth of July, therefore, Fremont and his mounted riflemen arrived at Monterey and a conference took place between him and Sloat.[21] When Sloat learned that Fremont was acting on his own authority, he dismissed both Fremont and his men, refusing to muster the unit in the service of the United States.[22]

On the fifteenth of July the United States frigate "Congress" with Commodore Robert F. Stockton aboard, arrived at Monterey. The tired and ailing Sloat now saw an opportunity to be relieved of his command, a request he had made to the Navy Department months before. Accordingly, therefore, Sloat turned over his command to Stockton on July 23, 1846. Six days later Sloat transferred his pennant to the "Levant" and sailed for the east coast.[23]

A completely different attitude was now assumed by the new commander toward the occupation of California. Possessing no further instructions than those he received from his predecessor,[24] Stockton decided to extend his activities in California. He accordingly re-interpreted the spirit of Sloat's orders to mean a more vigorous policy in Califor-

---

[21] Deposition of John C. Fremont, Washington, Feb. 28, 1848, *U.S. Gov. Doc. Ser. 512,* p. 75.

[22] *Ibid.:* Thomas O. Larkin, Monterey, to Fremont, Monterey, July 24, 1846, in George P. Hammond, ed., *The Larkin Papers,* p. 158.

[23] Sloat, Flagship "Levant," to Bancroft, Washington, July 31, 1846, *U.S. Gov. Doc. Ser. 493,* p. 641.

[24] See above, pp. 43-44.

COMMODORE ROBERT F. STOCKTON
United States military governor of California
from July 1846 to January 1847.
From Walter Colton's *Deck and Port*.

COMMODORE JOHN D. SLOAT
In 1846 he ordered the American flag raised at Monterey
on June 9, and served as military governor until July.
Courtesy of the Bancroft Library.

BRIGADIER GENERAL STEPHEN W. KEARNY
Commander of the First Dragoons of the United States Army, and
served as military governor of California, January to May 1847.
From V. M. Porter, *Kearny and Conquest of California*.

nia. This meant an immediate campaign to bring the entire province of California under American control.

Upon assumption of authority in California, Stockton issued a proclamation on July 28. The influence of Captain Fremont and Lieutenant Archibald H. Gillespie [25] is clearly noticeable both in tone and substance in this proclamation. Stockton began with a complete denunciation of the Mexican government and its aggression against the United States. He censured Military Commandant Don Jose Castro for his aggressive attitude toward Fremont and his topographical engineers. Military possession was ordered of both San Francisco and Monterey because of repeated outrages and "scenes of rapine, blood, and murder." More abuse was then heaped upon Castro who was called a usurper and practically a thief and traitor. In closing, the proclamation read :

> The commander in chief does not desire to possess himself of one foot of California for any other reason than as the only means to save from destruction the lives and property of the foreign residents, and citizens of the territory who have invoked his protection. As soon, therefore,

---

[25] Lieutenant Archibald Hamilton Gillespie of the United States Marine Corps was ordered by the government early in 1846 to deliver some important sealed documents to U.S. Consul Thomas O. Larkin in San Francisco. His mission and identity were to be completely secret; therefore he travelled as a merchant. After delivering the documents to Larkin, he sought out John C. Fremont and his Topographical Engineers, who were then leaving California, and delivered some letters to him. Later Gillespie and Fremont were associated with the Bear Flag Revolt.

as the officers of the civil law return to their proper duties, under a regularly organized govt., and give security for life, liberty and property alike to all, the forces under my command will be withdrawn, and the people left to manage their own affairs in their own way.[26]

As a consequence of the proclamation the Californians became confused, frightened and angered. Sloat's proclamation of a few weeks before expressed friendship and cordiality. Now, suddenly, and for no apparent reason Stockton adopted a "get tough" policy. Sloat, however, must have been aware of some of Stockton's plans, especially the mustering into the United States' service of Fremont's battalion,[27] for this occurred while Sloat was still in California.[28] But apparently Sloat was too tired and ill to protest. Stockton's proclamation, however, brought Sloat to his feet. In a letter to the Secretary of the Navy, dated August 10, 1846, Sloat stated:

The enclosed letter and address of Commodore Stockton to the people of California was handed me by him after the "Levant" was under way leaving the bay of Monterey; I threw it on my desk and did not read it until this moment.

---

[26] Proclamation to the people of California, R. F. Stockton, Monterey, July 28, 1846, MSS "Archibald H. Gillespie Collection," Special Collections Library, Univ. of Calif. at Los Angeles.

[27] Stockton at this time commissioned Fremont and Gillespie a major and a captain respectively, in the California Battalion. Some doubt has existed as to the official service equivalents to these commissions. Stockton offered this explanation: "I call it a Naval Battalion because it was not brought into service under the laws of the army." This would mean that these men held commissions in the Marine Corps.

[28] Sloat sailed from Monterey on July 29.

It does not contain my reasons for taking possession of or my views or intentions towards the country; consequently it does not meet my approbation. My reasons, views, and intentions, are contained in my proclamation, promulgated on the 7th of July at the hoisting of the American standard at Monterey.[29]

Stockton now turned his attention to the conquest of southern California, which he accomplished by ordering Fremont to San Diego, while he sailed for San Pedro. In a joint operation that followed, Fremont came north from San Diego, and Stockton's forces marched into Los Angeles on August 13 unopposed.[30]

Another proclamation was issued four days later in which Stockton was guilty in inaccuracies concerning the status of California.

The territory of California now belongs to the United States, and will be governed as soon as circumstances may permit, by the officers and laws, similar to those by which other territories of the United States are regulated and protected.[31]

Furthermore it was proclaimed that the commander in chief (Stockton) would be the governor, and military law (martial law) would

[29] Sloat, Flagship "Levant," to Bancroft, Washington, Aug. 10, 1846, *U.S. Gov. Doc. Ser. 537,* p. 1034.

[30] R. F. Stockton, Los Angeles, to Bancroft, Washington, Aug. 28, 1846, *U.S. Gov. Doc. Ser. 520,* p. 265.

[31] California did *not* belong to the United States, and it was held only as occupied enemy territory. Only after the Treaty of Guadalupe Hidalgo did California legally belong to the United States. Proclamation, R. F. Stockton, Aug. 17, 1846, Los Angeles, N. A. Microfilm 89, roll no. 33.

prevail.[32] In a separate address to the people, on the same date, Stockton outlined the civil (military)[33] government he planned to establish, in which he provided for a governor, secretary and a legislative council.[34]

By August 22, Commodore Stockton indicated that he planned to withdraw as soon as he could safely do so and turn over the governorship to Fremont, with Archibald Gillespie as secretary.[35] The reason for his withdrawal, he claimed, was to protect American commerce in the Pacific. He also considered the possibility of new victories in the war in Mexico.[36] He scheduled, therefore, an interview with Fremont on October 25 to carry out his plans of turning the government over to him.[37]

Events in Los Angeles, however, were to prevent Fremont's ascendency to the governorship at this early date. On September 24, largely because of Archibald Gillespie's indiscretions and arbitrary rule in Los Angeles, the southern portion of California suddenly flamed in revolt against him.[38]

[32] Curfews and other unpleasant restrictions associated with martial law were instituted, which were particularly ill-suited to Hispanic culture. *Ibid.*

[33] The term civil government was misused by the military commanders. Actually they meant military government.

[34] Stockton, Los Angeles, to Bancroft, Washington, Aug. 28, 1846, N. A. Microfilm 89, roll no. 33.

[35] Gillespie had been appointed military commander of southern California with headquarters at Los Angeles.

[36] Stockton, San Diego, to Bancroft, Washington, Nov. 23, 1846, N. A. Microfilm 89, roll no. 33.

[37] Stockton, Los Angeles, to Fremont, Los Angeles, Aug. 24, 1846, *U.S. Gov. Doc. Ser. 493*, p. 675.

Four days later Gillespie and his men were forced to accept terms offered by Juan Flores, who had assumed the leadership of the California forces. A messenger, Juan Flaco (John Brown), was dispatched by Gillespie to Monterey and covered the distance of four hundred and sixty miles in fifty-two hours – a remarkable performance. After resting three hours, Brown traveled another hundred and forty miles to San Francisco where he delivered the dispatch to Stockton.[39]

Elements of discontent soon manifested themselves in open revolt in the northern area also, although there seems to be little evidence to connect this with the movement in Los Angeles. The alcalde at Yerba Buena, Washington Bartlett, and several other Americans were again "purchasing" supplies from the different ranchos by merely taking what they wanted. The angered rancheros, therefore, on December 20, seized them and decided to hold them as hostages. According to the alcalde at Monterey, Walter Colton,

> The Californians stated that they had taken up arms, not to make war on the American flag, but to protect themselves from the depredations of those, who under the color of the flag, were plundering them of their cattle, horses and grain. . .[40]

They were ready to return to their homes, how-

[38] Juan Flores Proclamation, Oct. 1, 1846, N. A. Microfilm 89, roll no. 33; Stephen Clark Foster, "Alcalde of Los Angeles, 1847-1849," MSS in Bancroft Library, Univ. of Calif., Berkeley, Calif.

[39] Walter Colton, *Three Years in California*, pp. 64-5.

[40] *Ibid.*

ever, and abandon any further hostilities, if assurance was given them that these acts of lawless violence would stop.

Stockton at once made plans for the reconquest. He sent troops to San Pedro and with another company of men sailed for San Diego. Captain William Mervine in command of the "Savannah" arrived in San Pedro on October 6, and, with Captain Gillespie, attempted the recapture of Los Angeles.[41] Their advance was stopped at Dominguez Ranch in an engagement with the Californians which resulted in the loss of a dozen Americans killed and a second retreat toward San Pedro.[42] Stockton arrived in San Diego two weeks later, after a hasty reconnaissance of the Los Angeles area had resulted in the postponement of the plans to reoccupy it.[43]

San Diego, successfully reoccupied by the Americans, became Stockton's headquarters as weeks went by while plans were revamped. Early in December he received word of the arrival of General Stephen Watts Kearny with a portion of his original army from Santa Fe, having traveled across the most barren and inhospitable area of the southwest.[44] Major Fremont, now Lieutenant Colonel of the California Battalion, in the meantime, had been strengthening his forces by recruit-

---

[41] Wm. H. Mervine, San Pedro, to Stockton, Oct. 9, 1846, N. A. Microfilm 89, roll no. 33.

[42] *Ibid.*

[43] Stockton, San Diego, to George Bancroft, Washington, Nov. 23, 1846, N. A. Microfilm 89, roll no. 32.

[44] See above, p. 39.

ing men in the northern area around Monterey, and also making preparations to advance southward toward Los Angeles.[45]

After having successfully conquered New Mexico and established a working civil government, General Kearny began his overland march to California. Orders from the War Department had specifically determined this move.

> When you arrive at Santa Fe with the force already called, and shall take possession of it, you may find yourself in a condition to garrison it with a small part of your command, (as the additional force will soon be in that place,) and with the remainder press forward to California.[46]

At present-day Socorro, New Mexico, Kearny met Kit Carson who had dispatches from Commodore Stockton to the Secretary of the Navy stating that California was firmly in the control of United States forces. Assuming this to be the truth, Kearny sent three companies of men, roughly two hundred, back to Santa Fe. Turning over Stockton's dispatches to his guide, Thomas Fitzpatrick, with orders to proceed to Washington, Kearny went on to California, with Carson directing the way. When the detachment arrived at Warner's Ranch, their fears that all was not well in California,[47] were confirmed. On their march to San

---

[45] Stockton, San Diego, to Bancroft, Washington, Nov. 23, 1846, N. A. Microfilm 89, roll no. 33.

[46] Marcy, Washington, to Kearny, June 3, 1846, *U.S. Gov. Doc. Ser. 573*, p. 237.

[47] They had heard rumors to this effect from the Indians at the Colorado River.

Diego to meet with Stockton they encountered a small but able force of Californians at San Pasqual, where on December 6 the bloodiest battle of the conquest was fought. The Americans retained the battlefield but suffered almost eight times as many casualties as did the Californians. Finally under an escort of two hundred sailors and marines, sent out by Stockton, Kearny and his battle-weary battalion arrived safely at San Diego.[48]

Some three weeks went by, after Kearny's arrival in San Diego, before any action was undertaken to reconquer Los Angeles and Santa Barbara. Word had been daily expected from Fremont in the north that he was prepared for this joint offensive. Finally on December 29, Kearny and Stockton marched their forces out of San Diego towards Los Angeles. A dispatch had been forwarded the day before to Fremont notifying him of the offensive and urging him to begin his movement southward. Meanwhile in the south a hastily assembled force which consisted of Stockton's barefooted sailors and marines and fifty-seven of Kearny's dragoons, moved slowly northward.[49]

Command of this unit proved to be a touchy matter, resulting in a future conflict between General Kearny and Commodore Stockton. At this time, however, in order to present a united front against the enemy, General Kearny accepted the

[48] W. H. Emory, Dec. 6, 1846, *U.S. Gov. Doc. Ser. 517*, pp. 108-10. Kearny's forces suffered 18 fatalities.

[49] Stockton, San Diego, to Bancroft, Feb. 5, 1847, *U.S. Gov. Doc. Ser. 531*, p. 31.

post as second in command of the unit while Stockton assumed the position of commander in chief.[50]

As the forces of Stockton and Kearny pushed northward, the California forces under Flores retreated towards Los Angeles. In the meantime Fremont had begun his movement southward from Monterey and entered Santa Barbara, where in a dramatic eleventh hour pardon he spared the life of Jesús Pico, chief of the local insurgents. Continuing southward, Fremont came upon California forces at Rancho Cahuenga near San Fernando.[51]

The Stockton-Kearny column, meanwhile, had on January 8 and 9, 1847, engaged the Californians in battle at the San Gabriel River. A last ditch effort was undertaken by Flores to prevent the Americans from crossing this river.[52] The crossing was, however, successfully made and the California forces were sent retreating to Pasadena. The way to Los Angeles was now open and on the next morning, January 10, 1847, the Stockton-Kearny column entered Los Angeles and once more raised the flag in that city, a little over three months after it had been lowered upon Gillespie's capitulation.[53]

Flores realized at this time that it was useless to

---

[50] Testimony of Stockton, Dec. 9, 1847, *U.S. Gov. Doc. Ser. 507*, p. 191.

[51] Edwin Bryant, *What I Saw In California*, p. 358; William Streeter, "Recollection of William A. Streeter, 1843-1878," *California Historical Society Quarterly*, XVIII (June, 1939) 164.

[52] W. H. Emory, *U.S. Gov. Doc. Ser. 517*, p. 119.

[53] *Ibid.*

resist any longer. He had attempted to negotiate
some sort of reasonable peace with Stockton, but
had been faced with only the prospect of being shot
as a rebel if he were caught.[54] Flores, therefore,
turned over the command to Andrés Pico, and left
for Mexico.

Fremont, upon observing the California forces
at San Fernando, decided to use the services of his
newly-made friend, Jesús Pico. Pico was immediately dispatched to the Californian camp to per-
suade his brother, Andrés Pico, of the futility of
continuing the war.[55] He urged Andrés to surrender to his *savior,* and, thereupon, outlined the
generous and magnanimous nature of Fremont.
Doubtless the possibility was considered that sur-
rendering to Fremont might lead to less severe
terms. Accordingly on January 13, 1847, Fremont
met with the remnant of the defeated California
forces at a deserted rancho on the Cahuenga plain
and entered into the Capitulation of Cahuenga.[56]

A changed Fremont participated in this capitulation, for the former "fire-eater" of the Bear Flag
Revolt and the California Mounted Battalion now
adopted a policy of conciliation. Perhaps he attempted to undo the ruthless acts of his previous
career in California. At any rate, under the terms
of this agreement the insurgents were free to go

---

[54] Jose M. Flores, Los Angeles, to [Stockton] Jan. 1, 1847, N. A.
Microfilm 89, roll no. 33.

[55] Bryant, *What I Saw in California,* p. 374.

[56] Articles of Capitulation, Jan. 13, 1847, *U.S. Gov. Doc. Ser. 531,*
pp. 22-3.

home upon giving up their arms. All prisoners were released including those on parole, and they were guaranteed protection of life and property and were excused from taking the oath of allegiance while the war with Mexico existed. Also the Californians were free to leave the country if they wished.[57] Finally all were pardoned, even those who had violated the parole, which meant that Juan Flores would be protected under the terms of this treaty.[58]

Upon receipt of the terms of the capitulation at Cahuenga, Stockton was disturbed at the presumption of Fremont to negotiate such a treaty in the absence of the senior military officer. Seemingly Stockton was also disturbed at the clause pardoning all who had violated the parole.[59] Fremont's motives seem clear in light of subsequent events. Since he was more or less promised the governorship by Stockton, upon his departure, Fremont desired popularity and prominence among the Californians, and this he hoped to attain by his conciliatory nature.[60] After more serious reflection, however, Commodore Stockton decided that the peace of the province was more important than revenge or protocol.[61]

The clumsy and incompetent management of military affairs resulted in a needless and unpleas-

[57] *Ibid.*   [58] *Ibid.*

[59] Stockton, Los Angeles, to Bancroft, Washington, Jan. 15, 1847, *ibid.,* p. 21.

[60] See above, pp. 56-57.

[61] Stockton, Los Angeles, to Bancroft, Washington, Jan. 15, 1847, *U.S. Gov. Doc. Ser. 531,* p. 21.

ant chapter in the history of the American conquest of California – the Kearny-Stockton controversy. Many factors contributed to it; the poor line of communication, the confusing and contradictory orders, and the passion for personal glory on the part of some military commanders.

The presence, for example, of General Stephen Watts Kearny in California immediately made Commodore Stockton apprehensive. He felt he was to be replaced. His anxiety over the possible loss of command in California is evidenced by Stockton's reluctance to send forces to assist Kearny prior to the battle at San Pasqual.[62] Moreover his readiness to have a brigadier general serve under a colonel, which was Stockton's equivalent army rank, shows his unbounded ambition.

Whereas the lack of specific orders greatly restricted his predecessor, Stockton felt this condition gave him the needed latitude to implement his plans. He, therefore, lacked official sanction for most of his activities in California. The conquest, the establishment of "civil government" and the appointment of Fremont as governor were undertaken by Stockton without authority from Washington.[63] Yet in many ways he anticipated the government's wishes. Unhappily, however, he did not possess the instructions of July 12, 1846, which authorized the establishment of "civil govern-

---

[62] George W. Ames, ed., "A Doctor Comes to California," C.H.S.Q., XXI, p. 337.

[63] Testimony of Stockton, Dec. 9, 1847, *U.S. Gov. Doc. Ser. 507*, p. 197.

ment." [64] His testimony at the Fremont court-martial bears this out.

> I think I received no other instructions, except those Commodore Sloat turned over to me and some others received by Mr. Mase; afterwards the orders went to Commodore Shubrick or Biddle, and if sent to me were only sent through courtesy. I have no recollection of having received these instructions of the 12th of July, my right to establish the civil government was incident to conquest and I formed the government under the law of nations. [65]

On the other hand, General Kearny had specific orders concerning the conquest and the establishment of "civil government" in California. [66] In point of fact, his orders of June 3, 1846, specifically outlined the government's wishes.

> Should you conquer and take possession of New Mexico and Upper California, or considerable places in either, you will establish temporary civil governments therein – abolishing all arbitrary restrictions that may exist, so far as it may be done with safety.
>
> It is expected that the naval forces of the United States which are now, or will soon be in the Pacific, will be in the possession of all the towns on the seacoast, and will cooperate with *you* in the conquest of California. [67]

Despite his knowledge of Kearny's orders, Stockton refused to relinquish his authority. [68]

In explaining his highhanded action in Califor-

---

[64] *Ibid.*   [65] *Ibid.*

[66] Marcy, Washington, to Kearny, June 3, 1846, *U.S. Gov. Doc. Ser. 573*, p. 6.

[67] *Ibid.*

[68] Testimony of Stockton, Dec. 7, 1848, *U.S. Gov. Doc. Ser. 507*, p. 189.

nia, Stockton claimed that he repeatedly offered the supreme command to the General but he declined it.[69] It was, however, Stockton's opinion:

> That under the circumstances that existed I was entitled to retain the position in which I was placed as commander in chief. . .[70]

Yet according to the 1825 edition of the General Regulations of the Army, which was in use at this time, Stockton was clearly outranked by Kearny.

> 24.   The military officers of the land and sea services of the United States shall rank together as follows; 1. a lieutenant of the Navy with captains of the Army. 2. a master commandant with majors. 3. a captain of the Navy, from the date of commission with Lt. Colonels. 4. five years thereafter, with colonels. 5. ten years thereafter, with Brigadier-generals; and   6. 15 years after the date of his commission with major generals. But, should there be created in the navy the rank of rear admiral, then such rank only shall be considered equal to that of major general.
>
> 25.   Nothing in the preceding paragraph shall authorize a land officer to command any United States vessel or navy yard; nor any sea officer to command any part of the army on land; neither shall an army officer of the services have a right to *demand* any compliment, on the rank from an officer of the other service.[71]

It is difficult to understand under what "existing circumstances" could Commodore Stockton, whose relative army rank was that of colonel, command a brigadier general. General Kearny gave his

---

[69] *Ibid.*   [70] *Ibid.,* p. 190.
[71] Winfield Scott, Washington, to C. Q. Tompkins, July 20, 1846, *U.S. Gov. Doc. Ser. 520,* pp. 246-47.

reasons for not immediately pressing for the supreme command of California as being his inad-
equate army forces and the deference due to
Stockton.[72] Since the Commodore was in command
of the Pacific squadron and had a large force of
sailors and marines ready to employ in the conquest of California it was deemed unwise by
Kearny to insist on relieving him of command.[73]
It seems almost presumptuous on the part of Commodore Stockton to "offer" the command to
Kearny who would appear to be the automatic
successor to the supreme command. And yet by
rightful interpretation Kearny realized the supreme command in California would entail the
management of civil affairs, which his meager
force could not hope to assume. It was hardly
possible for him to occupy the main population
centers of the province and hope to maintain order
with less than a hundred troops in his command.
Had he accepted Commodore Stockton's offer to
assume the top command in California, the soldiers
and sailors of Stockton's forces would be serving
under Kearny as volunteers, subject to being withdrawn at any time at the Commodore's command.
The California Battalion under Fremont at a later
time refused to serve under Kearny despite the fact
that orders from Washington had commanded it.[74]
Therefore, Kearny would have been placed in an

---

[72] Testimony of Kearny, Jan. 8, 1848, *U.S. Gov. Doc. Ser. 507*, p. 322.

[73] *Ibid.*

[74] Fremont, Los Angeles, to Kearny, Los Angeles, Jan. 17, 1846, *ibid.*, p. 6.

extremely critical situation if volunteer forces serving under him would have suddenly been withdrawn. It seems prudent on his part that he refused
the supreme command in California until proper
reinforcements arrived to strengthen his position.

In the march of the "Stockton-Kearny forces" to
Los Angeles, Kearny accepted the secondary position of aide-de-camp to Commodore Stockton as a
temporary expedient.[75] But, in order to make his
official position known, and possibly to avert any
future conflict, Kearny submitted his orders of
June 3 and 18 to Stockton. The Commodore's
reply vaguely sidestepped the main issue and informed Kearny that he had anticipated the government's wishes and implied that he was now in
control.[76] Stockton's letter stated:

> DEAR GENERAL, With my best thanks, I return to
> you the dispatches from the War Department, addressed
> to you, which you did me the honor to allow me to read.
> I also sent copies of some of my letters, that you may see
> how far the wishes of the government have been anticipated
> and accomplished by the forces under my command.[77]

In later conversations General Kearny suggested
that these instructions meant that the civil affairs
should come under his command, to which Stockton later claimed:

> This, of course, amazed me, because I had more than

---

[75] Testimony of Kearny, Jan. 8, 1848, *ibid.,* p. 322.

[76] Stockton, Los Angeles, to Kearny, Dec. 16, 1846, *U.S. Gov. Doc.
Ser. 531,* p. 31.

[77] *Ibid.*

was the fact that Kearny had recognized Stockton both as governor and as commander-in-chief as late as January 17. Kearny stated, however, that this was done only because Stockton was "acting" in the said position.[84]

Several heated letters were exchanged, and Stockton then on January 16, 1847, dismissed Kearny with these words:

> I will only add, that I cannot do anything, nor desist from doing anything or alter anything on your demand; which I will submit to the president and ask for your recall – in the meantime you will consider yourself suspended from the command of the forces in this place.[85]

It is difficult to understand what Stockton meant by "in this place" for although he was within his rights to dismiss Kearny as a volunteer from his battalion, he had absolutely no authority to order him out of California. Realizing the hopelessness of the situation, Kearny, in a letter the following day, stated that he and his troops were leaving Los Angeles. He explained:

> I must for the purpose of preventing a collision between us & possibly a civil war in consequence of it, remain silent for the present, leaving with you the great responsibility of doing that for which you have no authority, & preventing me from complying with the president's orders.[86]

Stockton had on January 15 sent a rather lengthy

---

[84] *Ibid.*

[85] Stockton, Los Angeles, to Kearny, Los Angeles, Jan. 16, 1847, *U.S. Gov. Doc. Ser. 531,* p. 29.

[86] *Ibid.* Kearny, Los Angeles, to Stockton, Los Angeles, Jan. 17, 1847, N. A. Microfilm 89, roll no. 33.

letter to Secretary of the Navy Bancroft outlining his accomplishments in California.[87] He stated that the territory of California was peaceful again and that civil government had been established in the areas where the insurgents had interrupted it. He took the time to mention General Kearny's "defeat" at San Pasqual and his explanation of the disagreement with Kearny. Finally he remarked that he intended to withdraw from California and that he planned to turn over the governorship to John C. Fremont.[88]

On January 15, 1847, Fremont entered Los Angeles with four hundred men in his California Battalion. Kearny, being aware of Stockton's intentions to appoint Fremont governor,[89] sent Fremont a letter to test his loyalty. Fremont was instructed by Kearny not to make any organizational changes in the California Battalion. A copy of the Secretary of War Marcy's instructions of June 18, 1846, to Kearny were also forwarded to Fremont at this time.[90] These stated:

> Since my last letter, it has been determined to send a small force around Cape Horn to California. The arms, cannon, and provisions to be sent to the Pacific, will be accompanied by a company of the regular army. Arrangements are now on foot to send a regiment of volunteers by

---

[87] Stockton, Los Angeles, to Bancroft, Washington, Jan. 15, 1847, N. A. Microfilm 89, roll no. 33.

[88] *Ibid.*

[89] This information was included in the dispatch Kit Carson was taking to Washington when he was intercepted by Kearny in New Mexico; see above, p. 59.

[90] Marcy, Washington, to Kearny, June 18, 1846, *U.S. Gov. Doc. Ser. 573*, p. 240.

sea. These troops, and such as *may be organized in Upper California, will be under your command.*[91]

The governorship of California must have been an item highly prized by Fremont, for it was the motivating factor that made him disobey the orders of, and display overt insubordination toward, his superior, General Kearny. Fremont was ready to support the person who could give the best offer as regards the governorship of California. Stockton had offered him the prize immediately;[92] Kearny on the other hand was vague.

In a meeting with Kearny on January 16, 1847, Fremont broached the subject of the governorship and the best commitment he could get from Kearny, who was anxious for the support of Fremont, was that he saw no objections to appointing Fremont governor and that he expected to leave in a few weeks.[93] The Stockton offer, of course, was more concrete. Fremont, therefore, continued in his insubordination. He signed a statement that he would continue his support of the Commodore until Kearny and Stockton could adjust the question of rank between themselves.[94] This, of course, proved his ruin at the subsequent court-martial.[95]

---

[91] *Ibid.*

[92] Stockton, Los Angeles, to Bancroft, Washington, Feb. 18, 1847, *U.S. Gov. Doc. Ser. 537,* p. 1044.

[93] Testimony of Kearny, Jan. 8, 1848, *U.S. Gov. Doc. Ser. 507,* p. 323.

[94] Fremont, Los Angeles, to Kearny, Los Angeles, Jan. 17, 1847, *ibid.,* p. 6.

[95] This written statement, plus the testimony of Kearny and other witnesses resulted in proving Fremont guilty of insubordination at the court-martial held in 1847-1848.

It does not seem quite clear how Fremont, an army officer, could have imagined that a naval officer could protect him from a charge of insubordination towards his superior officer. Perhaps he felt that his influential father-in-law, Senator Thomas H. Benton, would protect him.

On the same day Kearny, attempting to avoid any collision with the forces of Fremont and Stockton and avert any civil war, withdrew his dragoons to San Diego.[96] Having less than one hundred men under his command he decided to remain silent until reinforcements arrived. He communicated the state of affairs in California to Washington and awaited his day.[97]

Momentarily, at least, Fremont appeared to be the winner in this controversy, for on January 16, 1847, Commodore Stockton commissioned J. C. Fremont, Esq., Governor and Commander-in-Chief in California "by authority of the president and Congress of the United States of America, and by *right of conquest*." [98] It was also declared that on this date the province had become a territory of the United States.[99] As Secretary of State, Stockton appointed William H. Russell and also commissioned seven gentlemen who were to constitute a legislative assembly and were ordered to meet at Los Angeles on March 1.[100]

This conflict between Kearny, Stockton and

---

[96] Kearny, Monterey, to Marcy, Washington, Mar. 15, 1847, *U.S. Gov. Doc. Ser. 573,* p. 293.

[97] *Ibid.*

[98] Proclamation, Stockton, Jan. 16, 1847, "Gillespie Collection."

[99] *Ibid.*   [100] *Ibid.,* see below, p. 95.

Fremont perhaps could have been averted had methods of communications been what they are today. Although the government seemed vague in its early instructions to some of its military leaders in the Mexican War, the instructions of August 13 and November 5, to the senior naval officer in the Pacific, were rather explicit.[101] The orders of November 5, 1846, explained:

> The president has deemed it best for the public interest to invest the military officer commanding with the directions of the operations on land and with the administrative functions of government over the territory occupied by us.
>
> You will relinquish to Col. Mason, or to General Kearny if the latter shall arrive before you have done so, the entire control over these matters, and turn over to him all papers necessary for the performance of his duties.[102]

Unfortunately these orders were not received for several months. By that time, of course, Stockton was no longer in command in California.

Dragoons under Kearny moved to San Diego where they boarded a ship and arrived at Monterey on February 8, 1847.[103] At Monterey Kearny met with the newly-arrived Commodore W. Brandford Shubrick, who carried orders to succeed Commodore Stockton as commander of the Pacific Squadron. After reading Kearny's orders Shubrick recognized him as the commanding officer in Cal-

---

[101] J. Y. Mason, Washington, to Stockton, Nov. 5, 1846, *U.S. Gov. Doc. Ser. 520*, p. 248.

[102] *Ibid.*

[103] Kearny, Monterey, to R. Jones, Washington, Mar. 15, 1847, *U.S. Gov. Doc. Ser. 573*, pp. 283-84.

ifornia, Shubrick maintaining supreme authority in naval affairs.[104]

As Governor of California, Fremont issued a proclamation on January 22, 1847, which more or less reiterated the provisions of the Capitulation of Cahuenga and called for all former civil officers to resume their duties.[105] Actually for a period of time Fremont was the *de facto* Governor of California, although it does not seem his control extended for any distance beyond the city of Los Angeles. But during his short tenure as governor, Fremont managed to involve the government in debts totalling many thousands of dollars.[106]

Fremont's doom was sealed with the arrival of Colonel Richard Barnes Mason on February 12, 1847, bringing letters and orders up to November 5, 1846, from the federal government at Washington.[107] Kearny continued operations as governor at Monterey, and on March 1, he and Commodore W. Brandford Shubrick issued a joint circular promising good government and outlining the separation of duties of the Army and Navy forces in California.[108] Three days later Kearny issued his proclamation which was conciliatory in tone, and

[104] Proclamation to the People of California, Kearny, Mar. 1, 1847, Monterey, N. A. Microfilm 182, roll no. 1.

[105] *The Californian,* San Francisco, Feb. 6, 1847.

[106] Fremont borrowed money and purchased supplies on the credit of the United States. Eulojio de Celes and Antonio Jose Cos were the principal debtors. See various letters written by Fremont indebting the government, *U.S. Gov. Doc. Ser. 573,* pp. 370-73.

[107] Kearny, to Brig. Gen. R. Jones, Mar. 15, 1847, *ibid.,* p. 284.

[108] Circular, W. Bradford Shubrick and Kearny, Mar. 1, 1847, Monterey, N. A. Microfilm 82, roll no. 1.

once again reflected the true motives of the government of the United States.[109]

It will be noted that the proclamation mentions neither Fremont nor Stockton, making the implication that for the first time a government is to be established in California which has the official sanction of the United States government. An interview occurred between Kearny and Fremont on March 26 at which time Fremont was asked to obey the proclamation of March 1, 1847.[110] Stubborn to the last, Fremont took an hour to decide, and then replied in the affirmative.[111]

Colonel Mason was sent to Los Angeles two days later, clothed with both civil and military powers.[112] He also bore a letter from Kearny requesting Fremont to see that all unsettled accounts involving the government were properly verified.[113] After sending his orderly several times to Fremont's headquarters only to be refused entrance, Mason became extremely angered at this obvious affront. When Fremont finally arrived, a heated argument ensued resulting in a challenge. Although the date for the duel was not arranged, the weapons selected were doubled barreled shotguns.[114]

[109] *Ibid.*, Proclamation to the People of California, Kearny, Mar. 1, 1847, Monterey.

[110] Testimony of Kearny, Nov. 15, 1847, *U.S. Gov. Doc. Ser. 573*, p. 104.

[111] *Ibid.*

[112] Kearny, to R. B. Mason, Mar. 27, 1847, Monterey, *ibid.*, p. 292.

[113] Kearny, Monterey, to Fremont, Los Angeles, Mar. 27, 1847, *U.S. Gov. Doc. Ser. 507*, p. 34.

[114] Foster, "Alcalde of Los Angeles, 1847-1848," pp. 19-22. "As soon

Fremont was later asked to submit a list to the governor of any civil appointments made by him and any other official records that might be in his possession, but again Fremont proved recalcitrant.[115] He informed the governor on April 13, almost two weeks after his request, that any orders that remained had been forwarded to the federal government, and therefore he had nothing to turn over to the established command in California.[116]

With the appearance of General Kearny's proclamation on March 3, 1846, the period of stable military government actually begins. Not only were the instructions of the federal government now being carried out, but also the office of governor was unified in the person of General Kearny, thus helping to restore prestige to the military authorities in California.

as Pryor and myself were alone after the quarrel, Pryor remarked that he never saw so much fuss made about a whore; that early in the morning as he came up to town. he saw an old woman bring her daughter to Fremont's door. Fremont received her at the door and ordered the sentry to give admittance to no one until further orders.

"When Pryor returned by Fremont's house the mother was still sitting there, and Mason's orderly was just going back to Pryor's house, and that was the cause of the whole difficulty."

[115] R. B. Mason, Los Angeles, to Fremont, Los Angeles, April 12, 1847, U.S. Gov. Doc. Ser. 573, p. 308.

[116] Ibid., J. C. Fremont, Los Angeles, to R. B. Mason, April 13, 1847.

Military Government Reigns Supreme

Properly defined, the government of California, from the raising of the American flag at Monterey on July 7, 1846, to the inauguration of Peter H. Burnett as first elected governor of California, on December 18, 1849, can only be referred to as military. Despite the well-meaning instructions of Secretary of War William L. Marcy to General Stephen Watts Kearny shortly after the outbreak of the Mexican War relative to the establishment of civil government in New Mexico and California, and the various proclamations of California military governors pronouncing civil government in effect, the fact remains that California was under military rule.[1] During this entire period no steps were taken by Congress, which is the only branch of government authorized to institute civil government in the territories,[2] to establish any form of civil government in California.

The period of military control in California changed significantly after ratification of the peace treaty of Guadalupe Hidalgo which officially ended the Mexican War on May 30, 1848.[3] Up to

---

[1] W. L. Marcy, Washington, to Col. S. W. Kearny, Fort Leavenworth, June 3, 1846, *U.S. Gov. Doc. Ser. 520,* pp. 153-55.

[2] *U.S. Const.,* Art. IV, sec. 3, cl. 2.

[3] News of the treaty did not reach California, however, until August 6, 1848.

the treaty date California was in military possession of the United States as one of the incidents of
war. It was governed by the right of the belligerent
under the laws of war.[4] Once the treaty of peace
between the United States and Mexico was signed,
however, the status of California automatically
changed.[5] California now became a possession of
the United States and awaited Congressional action
as regards civil government. Greater national issues
involving slavery and its extension delayed the
passage of territorial or civil government for California.[6]

Territory is acquired by sovereign nations
either by settlement, conquest, or treaty. When the
American forces occupied California as hostile
territory and established a military government,
the commander was not limited by the Constitution in respect to measures taken against the inhabitants.[7] His only restraints were the orders of
his superiors, public opinion, his own conscience
and the laws and customs of war.[8] Although the
Treaty of Guadalupe Hidalgo did not terminate
military government, the fact that California was
a part of the United States did restrict the military
commander's authority. He was now limited by
the Constitution. Laws in conflict with the Constitution were illegal. Political laws, such as tariffs,

---

[4] See above, p. 15.

[5] *American Insurance Company* v. *Cantor* (1828). 1 Peters, 511.

[6] California was admitted into the union as a free state as a result
of the Compromise of 1850.

[7] *Dooley* v. *United States* (1901), 182 U.S., 222, 230.

[8] *Dow* v. *Johnson* (1879), 100 U.S., 166.

were also automatically extended to California,
but the municipal laws of the province, which were
not in conflict with the Constitution, remained in
force until changed by Congress.[9] Simply stated,
therefore, military rule in California prior to the
Treaty of Guadalupe Hidalgo was unrestrained,
but after this pact became more clearly defined.

When Commodore John D. Sloat formally occupied the Mexican Province of California on
July 7, 1846, his instructions from Washington had
been fulfilled. He had no further orders regarding
any other aspect of the occupation.[10] The government's plan, to establish a "civil government" or
functioning government as an effective means to
control California and thus claim it under the
principle of *uti possidetis*,[11] was unknown to him.
He doubtless was aware of the earnest desire of the
United States to gain possession of California and
the attempts made by Americans to seize the province. Others, also, knew the United States' unbounded desire for California. Admiral Frederick
Walpole, commander of the British squadron in
the Pacific noted:

> The war of the United States with Mexico no doubt
> justifies them in seizing any part of her territory they can;
> if the war itself can be justifiable, is another question; but
> for a long while they have been secretly intriguing for
> California, and that in a time of peace between the two
> countries.[12]

[9] *American Insurance Company* v. *Cantor* (1828), 1 Peters, 511.
[10] See above, pp. 41-43.   [11] See above, p. 43.
[12] Frederick Walpole, *Four Years in the Pacific in Her Majesty's Ship Collingwood*, II, p. 206.

Despite meager instructions, Sloat appeared to sense the desires of the government. His conciliatory policy towards the inhabitants, as well as his theory regarding the local administration, were completely in accord with the government's wishes, which were detailed in later dispatches.[13] In his occupation proclamation, Sloat invited the "judges, alcaldes and other civil officials to retain their offices and to execute their function" as before.[14]

During the sixteen days of Commodore Sloat's command in California, American occupation was only extended over the major settlements in the north. Military authority was understandably supreme, although Sloat attempted to gain the confidence of the natives.[15]

Captain John B. Montgomery on July 9, 1846, occupied Yerba Buena (San Francisco), raised the United States flag, and read Sloat's proclamation.[16] Lt. James W. Revere performed similar duties at Sonoma on the same day.[17] At Fort Sutter (Sacramento) the American flag was raised under the command of Lieutenant Edward M. Kern.[18] On the thirteenth of July, Thomas Fallon of San Jose

---

[13] George Bancroft, Washington, to J. D. Sloat, July 12, 1846, *U.S. Gov. Doc. Ser. 520*, pp. 238-45.

[14] To the Inhabitants of California, Sloat, Monterey, July 7, 1846, N. A. Microfilm 89, roll no. 32.

[15] *Ibid.*

[16] John B. Montgomery, San Francisco, to Sloat, Monterey, July 9, 1846. *U.S. Gov. Doc. Ser. 493*, pp. 649-50.

[17] Montgomery, San Francisco, to Commander Joseph B. Hale, San Francisco, Nov. 19, 1846, Bancroft Library Microcopy C-A 206, reel 1.

[18] Montgomery, San Francisco to Commodore John D. Sloat, Monterey, July 11, 1846, N. A. Microfilm 89, roll no. 32.

received a flag from Commodore Sloat which he raised before the "hoosgow" at San Jose.[19]

Little was done by Commodore Sloat in organizing the military government during his short stay. Several alcaldes who refused to serve under the American government, were replaced. In Monterey Surgeon Edward Gilchrist and Purser Rodman Price were appointed "justices of the peace," while at San Jose, John Stokes succeeded the native alcalde.[20] To lend support to Sloat's forces and to help maintain order a militia, largely composed of American civilians, was organized in Monterey under Purser Daingerfield Fauntleroy and in San Francisco under Vice-Consul William A. Leidesdorff.[21] But the extent of military control in California under Commodore Sloat did not extend beyond the four areas of Monterey, Yerba Buena, San Jose and Fort Sutter.

Although stating that he would "prefer being sacrificed for doing too much than too little," Commodore Sloat took virtually no steps as regards a central government in California. His lack of orders, as pointed out earlier, greatly curtailed his operations, and, after meeting with Consul Thomas O. Larkin and Captain John C. Fremont and discovering that they too had no further orders regarding operations in California, the cautious

---

[19] Sloat, Monterey, to Bancroft, Washington, July 21, 1846, N. A. Microfilm 89, roll 32.

[20] Walter Colton, *Three Years in California*, p. 17.

[21] Sloat, Monterey, Bancroft, Washington, July 21, 1846, N. A. Microfilm 89, roll 32. Leidesdorff was not in command of the militia but took the lead in organizing it.

Sloat chose the careful road of inaction.[22] By July 23 Robert F. Stockton relieved Sloat of his command in California and immediately embarked on a policy calculated to complete the occupation of the entire province.[23]

After surveying the situation in California and making tentative plans for its total occupation, Stockton on July 29 issued a proclamation to the people.[24] In reference to civil government, Stockton made a rather strange statement which implied that American control of California was only temporary.

> As soon, therefore, as the officers of the civil law return to their proper duties, under a regularly organized government, and give security for life, liberty, and property alike to all, the forces under my command will be withdrawn, and the people left to manage their own affairs in their own way.[25]

This, of course, ran counter to the government's desire to keep possession of California and claim it under the principle of *uti possidetis*. It seems unlikely that Stockton ever seriously considered implementing the governmental provisions he outlined in his proclamation. He, doubtless, used this to entice the native civil government employees, who had been resigning in the face of the new

---

[22] Colton, *Deck and Port*, pp. 390-91.

[23] Stockton, Monterey, to Bancroft, Washington, Aug. 28, 1846, *U.S. Gov. Doc. Ser. 520*, pp. 265-66.

[24] Address to the People of California, Stockton, July 29, 1846, "Gillespie Collection."

[25] *Ibid.*

American government, to resume their work and prevent the municipal units from crumpling.[26]

Once the southern section of California was under American control, Commodore Stockton issued another proclamation on August 17 in Los Angeles. This proclamation took an entirely different stand regarding the government in California. After stating that the commandante governor of California, José Castro, had been forced out of the country and that the sailors, marines, and California Battalion of Mounted Riflemen were securely in control of the province, Stockton turned to matters of government.[27]

> The flag of the United States is now flying from my commanding position in the territory, and California is entirely free from Mexican domination.
>
> The territory of California now belongs to the United States, and will be governed as soon as circumstances may permit, by officers and laws, similar to those by which the other territories of the United States are regulated and protected.
>
> But until the Governor, the Secretary and the Council are appointed and various civil departments of the government are arranged, military law will prevail, and the commander in chief will be the governor and protect the territory.
>
> In the meantime the people will be permitted and are now requested to meet in their several towns and depart-

[26] In light of his proclamation of August 17 (cited below), Stockton had no intention of turning the government over to the native Californians.

[27] Proclamation to the People of California, Stockton, Los Angeles, Aug. 17, 1846, *U.S. Gov. Doc. Ser. 493*, pp. 669-70.

ments, at such time and place as they may see fit to elect civil officers to fill the places of those who decline to continue in office, and to administer the laws according to the former usage of the territory. In all cases where they fail to elect, the Commander-in-Chief and Governor will make the appointments himself.

All persons of whatever religion or nation who faithfully adhere to the new government will be considered as citizens of the territory and will be zealously and thoroughly protected in the liberty of conscience, their person and property. No persons will be permitted to remain in the territory, who do not agree to support the existing government, and all military men who desire to remain, are required to take an oath, that they will not take up arms against it, or do, or say anything to disturb its peace.

Nor will any persons, come from where they may, be permitted to settle in the territory who do not pledge themselves to be in all respects obedient to the law which may be from time to time enacted by proper authorities of the territory.

All persons who without special permission, are found with arms outside of their houses, will be considered as enemies and will be shipped out of the country.

All thieves will be put to hard labor on the public works, and there kept until compensation is made for the property stolen.

The California battalion of mounted riflemen will be kept in the service of the territory, and constantly on duty to prevent and punish any aggression by the Indians or any other persons upon the property of individuals, or the peace of the territory — and California shall thereafter be so governed and defended as to give security to the inhabitants, and to defy the power of Mexico.

All persons are required as long as the territory is under

martial law to be within their houses from ten o'clock at
night until sunrise in the morning.

R. F. STOCKTON,   Commander-in-Chief
and Governor of the Territory of California
Ciudad de Los Angeles, Aug. 17, 1846.[28]

The most glaring misstatement in the proclamation is, of course, the reference that California
"now belongs to the United States." Only by treaty
with Mexico could the transfer of the territory
legally be made.[29] Regarding the meaning of the
terms "military law" and "martial law," used in-
terchangeably in this proclamation, it can be safely
assumed that Stockton meant military government.
Although aware of the wide powers of a military
commander in occupied enemy territory,[30] Stockton nevertheless overestimated his authority. He
had no power to terminate military government
nor organize a civil government in California;[31]
yet he provided for these two possibilities in his
proclamation.

Although military control was extended over the
local alcaldes, some municipal offices were filled
by election. Several days after the proclamation of
August 17 was issued, Stockton decreed September
15 as election day for the towns and districts in
California for "the purpose of electing the alcaldes
and other municipal officers for one year." [32] Theo-

---

[28] Ibid.   [29] See below, p. 121-22.

[30] Testimony of Stockton, Dec. 9, 1847, U.S. Gov. Doc. Ser. 507, p.
198.

[31] This is a congressional power. U.S. Const. Art. IV, sec. 3, cl. 2.

[32] Proclamation, Stockton, Aug. 2, 1846, "Gillespie Collection."

retically all alcalde districts were to hold elections, applying both to Stockton appointees and holdover Mexican alcaldes. This proclamation stated in part that "in places where no alcaldes have been appointed by the present government, the former alcaldes are authorized and required to hold the election." [33] The strong arm of military authority thus spread over the local level.

As governor and commander in chief of California, Commodore Stockton made various appointments to implement his projected "civil" government. It is interesting to note that, although Stockton proclaimed an election for local officials to be held on September 15, he conveniently made appointments in more strategic areas before the elections. Another point worthy of mention is that in most of the elections held on that date the incumbents, or the appointees of Stockton were re-elected to the posts.[34] At Santa Barbara, for example, Thomas M. Robbins was appointed as alcalde. In Los Angeles the commodore appointed two alcaldes, John Temple and Alexander Bell, while at San Bernardino a brother of the famous mountain man Antoine Robidoux, Louis, was appointed alcalde. A native Californian, José Francisco Ortega was one of the alcaldes appointed by Stockton in San Diego; the other was John Finch.[35]

---

[33] *Ibid.*

[34] This does not imply that the elections were engineered, for the incumbent normally has a decided advantage over his opponents. Colton and Bartlett were incumbents elected to office.

[35] Alcalde Appointments, Aug. 5, 1846, "Gillespie Collection."

In the north where Captain John B. Montgomery was in charge, several changes were made in the local administration. On August 12 having received "serious complaints . . . of the incompetency and indisposition" of the alcalde at San Jose, Don Pedro Chabolla, Montgomery appointed George Hyde to replace him.[36] Hyde's instructions were

> . . . to exercise the authority & superintend all the duties of the civil magistracy at the pueblo of San Jose and throughout its proper district; upon the principles of strict equity; and (as far as consistent therewith) in conformity with the laws and usages heretofore observed in the country.[37]

At Yerba Buena (San Francisco) Stockton appointed Lieutenant Washington A. Bartlett as alcalde.[38] His jurisdiction included the entire San Francisco district. On September 15 the election was held with over one hundred votes cast. Washington A. Bartlett was continued as alcalde and José de Jesús Noé elected second alcalde; John Rose, treasurer; and Peter T. Sherrebeck, collector.[39]

One of the first, and probably most important appointments, made by Commodore Stockton in California was that of Walter Colton as alcalde of Monterey.[40] A United States Navy chaplain, Col-

---

[36] Montgomery, San Francisco, to George Hyde, San Jose, Aug. 12, 1846, B. L. Microcopy C-A 206, reel 1.

[37] *Ibid.*

[38] William T. Sherman, *Memoirs,* p. 61.

[39] *The Californian,* Monterey, Sept. 26, 1846.

[40] Colton, *Three Years in California,* p. 17.

ton, succeeded Purser R. M. Price and Dr. Edward Gilchrist, who were appointed by Commodore Sloat.[41] Amazed at the wide powers of his office Colton stated:

> Today I enter on the duties of my office as alcalde of Monterey; my jurisdiction extends over an immense extent of territory, and over a most heterogeneous population. Almost every nation has, in some immigrant, a representative here — a representative of its peculiar habits, virtues, and vices. Here is the reckless Californian, the half wild Indian, the roving traveller of the west, the lawless Mexican, the licentious Spaniard, the scolding Englishman, the absconding Frenchman, the luckless Irishman, the plodding German, the adventurous Russian, and the discontented Mormon. All come here with the expectation of finding but little work and less law. Through this discordant mass I am to maintain order, punish crime, and to redress injuries.

In the elections of September 15, Colton received the public mandate as alcalde of the Monterey district, a post he had been filling by military commission for two months.[42] Within the jurisdiction of Monterey, "a space of 300 miles," he was virtually the final authority, receiving appeals from lesser tribunals in the area. Except for review by the military governor, Alcalde Colton's decision was final.[43]

Colton performed additional service, along with

---

[41] *Ibid.*, p. 19.

[42] *The Californian*, Monterey, Sept. 19, 1846.

[43] Colton, *op. cit.*, p. 19.

Robert Semple,[44] in the publication of the Monterey *Californian,* the first English-language newspaper in the province. A small printshop formerly
operated by a Roman Catholic monk in "printing
a few sectarian tracts," provided the necessary
materials for the composition of this newspaper.
Paper was obtained from a ship in the harbor, and
with the press and ink found in the shop, Colton
and Semple published the first copies of the *Californian.*[45] A visitor to Monterey during this time
made the following comments on the little weekly
periodical:

> There was also a little newspaper published weekly;
> for, with the usual enterprise of our countrymen, and
> their naturally saturnine dispositions, they have pounced
> upon a font of types, carefully secreted between the fount
> of the church, and instead of being applied to their original
> purpose of disseminating the authority of Mexican rulers,
> they were made to preach the true republican doctrine to
> all the unbelievers among the astonished Californians.
> The editor of this infantile journal was Dr. Semple, who
> although supposed to have been connected with the famous
> Bear Flag party, wielded the editorial pen with the same
> facility as his rifle, and merits all praise for having been
> the pioneer of civil and religious liberty in the country. I
> only trust the doctor will live to fill his ample pockets

[44] Semple, a colorful character, was prominent in the Bear Flag
Revolt and later in the Constitutional Convention. He was described
by his partner, Colton, as "an immigrant from Kentucky who stands
six feet eight in his stocking feet. He is in a buckskin dress, a foxskin
cap; is true with his rifle, ready with his pen and quick at the type
case." *Ibid.,* p. 32.

[45] *Ibid.*

with gold dust, even though they may be as lengthy as his legs or editorials.[46]

Although he had no orders regarding customs laws, Commodore Stockton realized that some modification should be made of the Mexican tariff regulation in force in California. Accordingly he established new customs laws for the province. All United States ships entered free of duty. Foreign vessels were charged tonnage duties at the rate of fifty cents per ton. Goods from foreign ports were taxed fifteen per cent ad valorum. To appraise goods for taxation, two disinterested persons were selected, one by the government authorities and the other by the owner of the goods.[47]

Shortly before the elections (September 12) Commodore Stockton brought California under closer military control by organizing it into military units.[48] The province was divided into three military sectors; each with a separate military commandant. The northern sector, which included the areas of Yerba Buena, San Jose, and Fort Sacramento (Sutter's Fort) was under the military command of Captain John B. Montgomery.[49] In the central sector, which included Monterey and environs, Lieutenant William A. Maddox was

[46] Lt. Henry A. Wise, *Los Gringos; or an Inside View of Mexico and California,* 82.

[47] Circular, Stockton, Los Angeles, Aug. 15, 1846, *U.S. Gov. Doc. Ser. 493,* p. 673.

[48] General Order, Stockton, Los Angeles, Sept. 2, 1846, *U.S. Gov. Doc. Ser. 531,* p. 8.

[49] Stockton, Monterey, to John Y. Mason, Washington, Feb. 18, 1847, *ibid.,* p. 1045.

appointed military commandant. The southern
sector, which included the area of Los Angeles,
San Diego, and Santa Barbara, was placed under
the command of Captain Archibald H. Gillespie.
To coordinate the activities of these three units, in
the event of rebellion, a military commandant for
the entire province of California was appointed.
Major Fremont, of the California Battalion was
selected for this post, but the supreme authority in
all matters in California, was, of course, the commander in chief and military governor, Commodore Stockton.[50]

Even before the elections took place Stockton
was formulating plans upon his leaving California
to turn over the governorship to Fremont. In a
dispatch to Fremont on August 24 he stated:

> I propose before I leave the territory to appoint you to
> be governor, and Capt. Gillespie the secretary thereof;
> and to appoint also a counsel of state, and all the necessary
> officers.[51]

By the end of the month, Stockton had drawn up
a constitution and dispatched it to Secretary of the
Navy George Bancroft.[52] Elaborately defining the
executive and legislative powers, this constitution
represented Stockton's efforts in establishing a civil
government in California. The constitution, how-

---

[50] *Ibid.*

[51] Stockton, Los Angeles, to Major Fremont, Los Angeles, Aug. 24,
1846, *U.S. Gov. Doc. Ser. 493,* p. 675.

[52] Stockton, Los Angeles, to Bancroft, Washington, Aug. 28, 1846,
U.S. Gov. Doc. Ser. 499, pp. 106-7.

ever, was neither published nor proclaimed [53] by Stockton in California; but it is interesting that he claimed credit for its implementation in his dispatch to Washington. He stated:

> I enclose to you several dispatches marked one to fourteen of which number six is the constitution by which you will see what sort of a government I have established, and how I am proceeding.[54]

Doubtless, Stockton was seeking the favor and approbation of his superiors.

The uprising in the southern section which seriously threatened the position of the Americans in California and which soon spread to other parts of the province, altered Stockton's plans regarding his departure and appointment of Fremont as governor. After the reconquest of the province, which was undertaken jointly by Stockton and the newly-arrived Brigadier General Stephen Watts Kearny,[55] Stockton, in face of specific orders from Washington naming Kearny as senior officer and governor of California, continued in his determination to name Fremont as governor. Accordingly, therefore, on January 16 Stockton sent commissions to Fremont as Governor and William H. Russell as Secretary of California.[56]

---

[53] The record shows no evidence that this constitution was ever made public. There appears to be no reason for Stockton's reluctance to put the constitution in force. It is possible that with the uprising and the period of reconquest, Stockton may have reconsidered and felt the military government as safest in guarding the United States' interest.

[54] *Ibid.*

[55] Kearny arrived at Warner's Ranch in California on Dec. 3, 1846.

Assumption of office had to await Stockton's departure from Los Angeles on the nineteenth.[57] By a proclamation issued on January eighteenth, a day before his departure, Stockton also established a council of seven members to act as a Legislative Council to the Governor. These members were Mariano Guadalupe Vallejo, David Spence, Juan Bautista Alvarado, Thomas O. Larkin, Eliab Grimes, Santiago Arguello, and Juan Bandini.[58] The proclamation had ordered the council to convene in Los Angeles on March 1; but, with Stockton's departure, interest in it suddenly declined. Members refused to serve and subsequent administrations saw no need for it. However, some sort of a precedent was established, for General Kearny was later called upon by the people of San Francisco and Sonoma to recognize duly elected members to a projected legislative council. Kearny's refusal to this proposal was short and to the point, and no more agitation in this regard appeared during his administration.[59]

As governor and commander in chief in California, Commodore Stockton succeeded in placing the entire province under his control and attempted

---

[56] Stockton, San Diego, to Bancroft, Washington, Jan. 22, 1847, N. A. Microfilm 89, roll no. 33. Stockton had intended to appoint Gillespie, secretary, but the latter chose to advance to Major in the California Battalion.

[57] *Ibid.*

[58] Proclamation, Stockton, Los Angeles, Jan. 18, 1847, "Gillespie Collection."

[59] Kearny, Monterey, to Edwin Bryant, Yerba Buena, Mar. 4, 1847, *U.S. Gov. Doc. Ser. 573*, p. 290.

to establish civil government. He left feeling confident that he had succeeded, for he considered the Fremont government a civil administration, which it was not. In a larger sense, however, Stockton succeeded in extending the military authority over the local units of government, thus establishing a policy followed by his successors.[60]

Assuming the governorship after Stockton left, Fremont proudly paraded his California Battalion in the streets of Los Angeles, and on January 22 issued a proclamation to the people of California. It stated in part:

> I do hereby proclaim order and peace restored to the country, and require the immediate release of all prisoners, the return of the civil officers to their appropriate duties, and as strict obedience of the military to the civil authority as is consistent with the security of peace and maintenance of good order where troops are garrisoned.[61]

This proclamation, as well as the changed attitude of Fremont regarding the Californians, resulted in increased popularity and support for his government. The *California Star* of February 9 highly praised the Governor and his proclamation.

> Glorious news. We have crowded out much other interesting matter today in order to make room for the entire news of the army in the south, and from the town of the Angels, the temporary seat of government for the territory. It will be seen by the accounts from below, that the enemies

---

[60] Stockton, San Diego, to Bancroft, Washington, Jan. 22, 1847, N. A. Microfilm 89, roll no. 33.

[61] *The Californian,* Monterey, Feb. 6, 1847.

of our country, have been entirely subdued — peace prevails throughout the territory — and that a civil organization has been commenced. This will be hailed with joy by every lover of this country and by every class of our citizens. The rigors of military law will no longer impede the civil operations of our citizens, and we trust it will never again be necessary to put it in force. The circular of Governor Fremont, which was forwarded to us by honorable Thomas O. Larkin for publication, will be read with interest. It is short and sweet, plain and to the point. It releases all prisoners throughout the country, does away with martial law, makes the military subservient to the civil authorities! We are gratified to find that our Civil Governor has been so prompt, in doing everything at present in his power, in relieving them of the unnecessary inconvenience which they have for some time past been laboring. We do not understand it to be the intention of the Governor to release any public prisoners. Those confined for crimes and misdemeanors committed as private individuals, will be retained in custody, and tried and punished by the laws of the country.[62]

Nothing of serious consequence was accomplished in the fifty-day tenure of Fremont as governor of California. People returned to their peaceful pursuits and all seemed quiet and happy in Los Angeles, the temporary capital of California.[63] Yet Fremont's administration was greatly weakened by the lack of available funds. Several questionable transactions were entered into by Fremont in order to obtain money for his government. Several thousand dollars were obtained by Fremont by issuing United States government notes

[62] *The California Star,* San Francisco, Feb. 9, 1847.
[63] Edwin Bryant, *What I Saw in California,* p. 400.

bearing three per cent interest per month.[64] An additional fifteen thousand dollars was also secured on the strength of government security with a promised premium of forty-five hundred dollars accruing to the lender.[65] Another crafty deal entered into by Fremont was the payment for six thousand head of cattle which were never delivered.[66] These "irregular activities" seemed to suggest in part that Fremont's administration was not free from the temptation of personal interest.

Besides orders for courts-martial, Fremont's official duties included the appointment of Don Santiago Argüello as collector of customs in San Diego and Don Pedro Carrillo at Santa Barbara.[67] The Mexican brig "Primavera" was granted a license by Fremont to "trade on any portion of the coast of California" with the same privileges as United States ships. This was immediately revoked by General Kearny when he assumed the governorship of California.[68] It seemed strange that this license be granted to a ship of a country with which the United States was still at war. Another peculiar act of Fremont was the purchase of White Island in San Francisco Bay for five thousand

---

[64] Fremont, Los Angeles, to Antonio Jose Cos, Los Angeles, Feb. 20, 1847, *U.S. Gov. Doc. Ser. 573*, p. 329.

[65] Robert J. Atkinson, Washington, to James Guthrie, Washington, Aug. 16, 1856, *U.S. Gov. Doc. Ser. 825*, p. 40.

[66] R. B. Mason, Monterey, to R. Jones, Washington, Oct. 9, 1847, *U.S. Gov. Doc. Ser. 573*, pp. 363-64.

[67] Fremont, Los Angeles, to Mason, Los Angeles, April 13, 1847, *U.S. Gov. Doc. Ser. 573*, p. 308.

[68] Kearny, Monterey, to James Biddle, Monterey, April 11, 1847, *ibid.*, p. 295.

dollars from Francis Temple. The five thousand dollars were to be paid as soon as funds were received from the United States. The reasoning behind this purchase is curious, for it bound the United States to pay five thousand dollars for property in an area which it held and governed only by right of military conquest under the law of nations.[69]

The pressing need for funds even prompted Fremont to dispatch a letter to Secretary of State Buchanan for financial assistance in maintaining the government in California. This letter shows Fremont's misconception concerning his position in California, for, as a military governor of occupied enemy territory, Fremont should have addressed the Secretary of War.[70]

When Commodore W. Branford Shubrick arrived in California on January 22, 1847, as a replacement for Commodore Stockton, Fremont dispatched a letter to him outlining the financial plight of the government in California.[71] He thereupon pointed out the necessity of a loan and asked the Commodore to grant him the required sum. Shubrick, who was not completely sure by what

[69] Fremont, Los Angeles, to Francis Temple, San Francisco, Mar. 2, 1847, *U.S. Gov. Doc. Ser. 507,* p. 12.

[70] W. L. Marcy, Washington, to Kearny, California, June 11, 1847, *U.S. Gov. Doc. Ser. 573,* pp. 249-51. Technically Fremont was still a military man holding a Lieutenant Colonelcy in the California Battalion, which had been mustered into the U.S. military forces by Stockton.

[71] Fremont, Los Angeles, to W. Branford Shubrick, Monterey, Feb. 7, 1847, *U.S. Gov. Doc. Ser. 507,* p. 10.

authority Fremont governed in California refused to grant the loan.[72]

Fremont's short-lived administration in California, which he and Stockton chose to refer to as civil government, appealed to many who soon regarded Fremont as the savior and protector of civil freedom in California. Yet, surprisingly little was done by Fremont in governmental matters, and, perhaps, that was the reason for his popularity; that is "the government rules best that rules least."

The transfer of control from Fremont to Kearny was anything but smooth as noted earlier. After meeting with Commodore Shubrick and agreeing on areas of control, Kearny quietly took charge of the government at Monterey on February 9. Fremont was allowed to continue in his insubordination until after the publication of Kearny's proclamation on March 1, 1847.[73]

When Commodore Stockton commissioned Fremont as governor and refused to recognize General Kearny's authority in California, Kearny and his dragoons left Los Angeles for San Diego, where he dispatched letters to Washington concerning the events in California, and planned to embark aboard the "Cyane" for Monterey. On the twenty-ninth the Battalion of Mormon Volunteers, which consisted of over three hundred men under the command of Lieutenant Colonel Philip St. George

---

[72] Kearny, Monterey, to R. Jones, Washington, Mar. 15, 1847, *U.S. Gov. Doc. Ser. 573*, p. 283.

[73] *Ibid.*, pp. 283-5.

Cooke, arrived in San Diego and reported to General Kearny. After ordering Cooke and the battalion to station themselves at "St. Louis Rey," Kearny and his 1st Dragoons left San Diego, reaching Monterey on the thirty-first.[74] A meeting was thereupon arranged between Kearny and Commodore Shubrick, who had arrived in Monterey on January 22, and it was decided, in view of more recent dispatches from Washington, that the controversy concerning the senior command in California should be dropped. Thereupon Shubrick recognized Kearny as senior military officer on land and himself assumed the position of leading naval officer in California.[75] A few days later, therefore, Kearny left on the "Cyane" for San Francisco, where he found Colonel Richard B. Mason of the 1st Dragoons, who had arrived on February 12. Kearny returned to Monterey with Mason where, on March 1, Commodore Shubrick and Kearny issued a joint circular. The circular proclaimed the division of authority in California, the governorship and land forces being under the command of Kearny and the naval forces and regulation of ports in the hands of Commodore Shubrick. On the same day Kearny issued his proclamation to the people of California as Governor.[76]

[74] *Ibid.*, p. 286.

[75] Circular, Shubrick and Kearny, Mar. 1, 1847, *U.S. Gov. Doc. Ser. 537,* p. 1071.

[76] Kearny, Monterey, to R. Jones, Washington, Mar. 15, 1847, *U.S. Gov. Doc. Ser. 573,* pp. 283-88.

PROCLAMATION TO THE PEOPLE OF CALIFORNIA

The President of the U.S. having instructed the under-signed to take charge of the civil government of Cal., he enters upon his duties with an ardent desire to promote, as far as he is able, the interests of the country and the welfare of its inhabitants. The undersigned has instructions from the President to respect and protect the religious institutions of Cal., and to see that the religious rights of the people are in the amplest manner preserved to them, the Constitution of the U.S. allowing every man to worship his Creator in such a manner as his own conscience may dictate to him. The undersigned is also instructed to protect the persons and property of the quiet and peaceable inhabitants of the country against all or any of their enemies, whether from abroad or at home; and when he now assures the Californians that it will be his duty and his pleasure to comply with those instructions, he calls upon them all to exert themselves in preserving order and tranquility, in promoting harmony and concord, and in maintaining the authority and efficacy of the laws. It is the wish and design of the U.S. to provide for Cal., with the least possible delay, a free government similar to that in her other territories; and the people will soon be called upon to exercise their rights as freemen, in electing their own representatives to make such laws as may be deemed best for their interests and welfare. But until this can be done, the laws now in existence, and not in conflict with the Constitution of the U.S. will be continued until changed by competent authority; and those persons who hold office will continue in the same for the present, provided they swear to support that Constitution, and to faithfully perform their duty. The undersigned hereby absolves all the inhabitants of Cal. from any further allegiance to the Republic of Mexico, and will consider them as citizens of the U.S. Those who remain quiet and peaceable will be respected in their rights, and protected in them. Should any take up arms against or oppose the government of this territory, or instigate others to do so, they will be considered as enemies, and treated accordingly. When Mexico forced a war upon the U.S., time did not permit the latter to invite the Californians as friends to join her standard, but compelled her to take possession of the country to prevent any European power from seizing upon it; and in doing so, some excesses and unauthorized acts were no doubt committed by persons employed in the service of the U.S., by which a few of the inhabitants have met with a loss of property. Such losses will be duly investigated, and those entitled to remuneration will receive it. California has for many years suffered greatly from domestic troubles; civil wars have been the poisoned fountains which have sent forth trouble and pestilence over her beautiful land. Now those fountains are dried up; the star-spangled banner floats over Cal.; and as long as the sun continues to shine upon her, so long will it float there over the natives of the land, as well as others who have found a home in her bosom; and under it agriculture must improve and the arts and sciences flourish, as seed in a rich and fertile soil. The Americans and Californians are now but one people; let us cherish one wish, one hope, and let that be for the peace and quiet of our country. Let us as a band of brothers unite and emulate each other in our exertions to benefit and improve this, our beautiful, and which soon must be our happy and prosperous, home. Done at Monterey, capital of Cal., first day of March, A.D. 1847, and in the 71st year of the independence of the U.S.

S. W. KEARNY, Brig.-Gen. U.S.A.,
and Governor of California.[77]

In tone the proclamation was inoffensively stern and yet friendly enough to continue the conciliatory attitude begun by Commodore Sloat. Con-

[77] Proclamation to the People of California, Kearny, Mar. 1, 1847, N. A. Microfilm 82, roll no. 1.

cerning the annexation of the province, Kearny
continued in the misconception of his predecessors.
Without using the word annexed, he virtually proclaimed California a part of the Union. Kearny
was more to blame than his predecessors, because
he had had instructions to refrain from such an
announcement. These instructions were sent by
Major-General Winfield Scott on November 3,
1846, and had already been received by Kearny.
This letter stated:

> As a guide to the civil governor of Upper California, in
> our hands, see the letter of June the 3d, (last) addressed
> to you by the Secretary of War. You will not, however,
> formally declare the province to be annexed. Permanent
> incorporation of the territory must depend on the govern-
> ment of the United States.[78]

Regarding the administration of military government under Kearny, little was done to change
what had already been established under Stockton
and Fremont. Alcaldes appointed or elected under
the Stockton administration were permitted to continue in their office. The only exception to this was
where naval officers were appointed to governmental posts. They were recalled by Commodore
James Biddle, the senior naval authority in the
Pacific.[79] Some young army officers rejoiced as

---

[78] Winfield Scott, Washington, to Kearny, 10th Military Dept., Nov.
3, 1846, *U.S. Gov. Doc. Ser. 520,* pp. 163-65.

[79] Commodore Biddle was Commander of the Pacific Squadron
which included all American squadrons in the Pacific Ocean. He did
not interfere with Commodore Shubrick's command of the North
Pacific Squadron. Biddle remained in California from March to July,
1847. One of the naval officers he recalled was Lt. Archibald Gillespie.

In addition to recommissioning his predecessor's appointees, Kearny appointed Lilburn W. Boggs to replace John H. Nash as alcalde in the district of Sonoma.[86] Edwin Bryant resigned as alcalde of the district of San Francisco and Kearny appointed George Hyde to replace him.[87] The Governor also figured prominently in several alcalde's judicial decisions. In the case involving the question of ownership of land, Kearny on April 27 overruled the alcalde of San Jose, John Burton, and stated:

> I have now to decree that you stay all further proceedings in this case until you hear further from me on the subject.[88]

In another case involving a military order given by Captain John Montgomery as commandant of San Francisco, Kearny again overruled the alcalde, the military remaining supreme.[89]

A clue to Kearny's opinion of military government in California is found in a letter sent to George W. Bellemy of Santa Clara. Bellemy apparently had suffered some injustices under the existing government and had written Kearny about them. Kearny's reply was courteous and sympathetic, but he pointed out that these hardships

---

[86] Kearny, Monterey, to John A. Nash, Sonoma, Mar. 3, 1847, *U.S. Gov. Doc. Ser. 573,* p. 290.

[87] Kearny, Monterey, to George Hyde, San Francisco, May 28, 1847, *ibid.,* p. 306.

[88] Kearny, Monterey, to John Burton, San Jose, April 27, 1847, *ibid.,* p. 301.

[89] Kearny, Monterey, to Edwin Bryant, San Francisco, *ibid.,* pp. 301-2.

occur until the establishment of permanent civil government. Kearny stated:

> During the existence of the present war between the United States and Mexico, there must of necessity arise many cases of great hardship and injustice, which for the time being are without remedy. This state of affairs is inseparable from a state of war, and your case, as represented by you, may be considered as one of that class. I sincerely hope that ere long the restoration of peace will lead to the establishment of a permanent civil government for this territory, which will secure to all their just rights.[90]

The amount of military support given municipal authorities is another indication of the superiority of the military government. In a case in which the alcalde of San Diego, Henry Delano Fitch, had some difficulty in enforcing his decrees, Kearny was immediately ready to furnish military support. In a letter to Fitch on April 27, Kearny informed him:

> I regret to learn that Mr. Warner refuses obedience to your decree. If he remain refractory, you are authorized to call upon the military officer most convenient to you for men to enforce your decree. This authority is also delegated to you in any other case in which the military may be required to give effect to your judicial acts.[91]

Full military support was ever present to help the local alcaldes enforce decrees not contrary to the orders of the military governor.

---

[90] Kearny, Monterey, to George W. Bellemy, Santa Clara, April 24, 1847, *ibid.*, p. 299.

[91] Kearny, Monterey, to H. D. Fitch, San Diego, April 27, 1847, *ibid.*, p. 302.

With the arrival of a regiment of New York Volunteers under the command of Colonel Jonathan Drake Stevenson in March and April of 1847, General Kearny's position in California was greatly strengthened. Companies from this regiment were sent to various cities in California to supplement the meager military forces existing there. The commander, Colonel Stevenson, was appointed by Kearny to replace Colonel Cooke as military commandant of the southern district. By the end of May, Kearny concluded that California was firmly under American control. He, therefore, appointed Colonel Mason as Governor of California on May 31 and returned overland to St. Louis.[92]

Almost immediately upon assuming the governorship of California, Colonel Mason was faced with the problem of asserting his authority in the local levels of government. The deposed alcalde of Sonoma, John H. Nash, chose to defy General Kearny's authority in appointing Lilburn W. Boggs as Nash's successor. Nash felt that his election on September 15 had placed him in a position beyond the control of the military governor in California. Accordingly, with the support of the people of Sonoma, Nash refused to turn his office over to Boggs.[93] When Colonel Mason received word of this affair he immediately dispatched a

[92] Kearny, Monterey, to J. D. Stevenson, Los Angeles, May 8, 1847, "Jonathan Drake Stevenson Collection," Univ. of Calif. at Los Angeles.

[93] John H. Nash, Sonoma, to Kearny, Monterey, April 28, 1847, "Archives of California, Unbound Documents, 1846-1850," Bancroft Library.

letter to Boggs authorizing him to secure the
assistance of the nearest military officer in assuming his office at Sonoma. In his letter to Boggs,
Colonel Mason took the opportunity to define his
theory of government in California. He said:

> This is a military government, and the supreme power,
> as you see, is vested in the senior military officer in the
> Territory. My instructions tell me that it is the duty of
> the executive to carry on the war with all the rights and
> subject to all the duties imposed by the law of nations, a
> code binding on both belligerents.
>
> The possession of portions of the enemy's territory,
> acquired by justifiable acts of war, gives to us the right of
> government during the continuance of our possession, and
> imposes on us a duty to the inhabitants who are thus placed
> under our domination.
>
> This right of possession, however, is temporary, unless
> made absolute by subsequent events. . .
>
> Pending the war, our possession gives us only such rights
> as the law of nations recognize; and the government is
> military, performing such civil duties as are necessary to
> the full enjoyment of the advantages resulting from the
> conquest, and to the due protection of the rights of persons
> and of property of the inhabitants.
>
> No political rights can be conferred on the inhabitants
> thus situated, emanating from the Constitution of the
> United States. That instrument established a form of gov-
> ernment for those who are within our limits, and owe
> voluntary allegiance to it, unless incorporated, with the
> assent of Congress, by ratified treaty or by legislative act,
> as in the case of Texas. Our rights over enemy's territory
> and our possession are such as the laws of war confer, and
> theirs no more than are derived from the same authority.[94]

[94] Mason, Monterey, to L. W. Boggs, Sonoma, June 2, 1847, *U.S.
Gov. Doc. Ser. 573,* pp. 317-18.

Captain John F. Brackett, commander of the military unit at Sonoma was called upon to assist Boggs.[95] The people of Sonoma immediately resented this military interference and Captain Brackett deemed it advisable, in view of his position as volunteer and his plans of settling in Sonoma, not to pursue the action any further. This greatly aroused the ire of Mason, who seemed ready to storm Sonoma and depose Nash personally. Coming to his aid, however, was Lieutenant William T. Sherman who volunteered to help install Alcalde Boggs. Under the cover of night Boggs and Sherman entered Sonoma, captured Nash and brought him to Monterey.[96] There it was explained to him that the government in California was military and the governor was supreme. The frightened and enlightened Nash admitted his mistake and agreed to surrender his office and his papers to Boggs. Colonel Mason then ordered his release and Alcalde Boggs was installed in his proper office.[97]

Although invested with wide powers, alcaldes were somewhat limited in their jurisdiction. Only Judges of First Instance (generally the senior alcalde of the district) could assume criminal jurisdiction. Faced with an increasing population and a consequent increase in crime, Colonel Mason found it necessary to extend the jurisdiction of the

---

[95] Mason, Monterey, to J. F. Brackett, Sonoma, June 2, 1847, N. A. Microfilm 82, roll no. 1.

[96] Sherman, *Memoirs,* I, p. 58.

[97] Mason, Monterey, to L. W. Boggs, Sonoma, July 22, 1847, N. A. Microfilm 82, roll no. 1.

alcalde courts. He decreed that all alcaldes could assume criminal jurisdiction, but in all cases involving one hundred dollars or more a jury consisting of "six good and lawful men" would have to be empaneled.[98] Decisions, moreover, involving capital punishment had to be reviewed by the governor. There were times as in a trial at San Jose, when the sentence was first carried out and then gubernatorial sanction asked.[99]

A case that could have caused some international complications, and which, curiously enough, was sanctioned by Governor Mason, involved the arrest and imprisonment of a British sea captain, a Captain David Dring, who was accused of receiving deserters from the United States Navy aboard his ship.[100] The Captain was tried in an alcalde court and on his refusal to pay the fine he was jailed. The British consul, James Alexander Forbes, communicated with the governor asking that the captain be released and the fine removed. Governor Mason, however, "finding that the fine had been imposed in a regular course of law" refused to commute the sentence.[101]

Occasionally Governor Mason found it necessary to appoint special tribunals to try more

---

98 Mason, Monterey, to [all Alcaldes], Dec. 29, 1847, "D. W. Norris Collection," Bancroft Library.

99 Mason, Monterey, to R. Jones, Washington, Dec. 27, 1848, N. A. Microfilm 82, roll no. 1.

100 H. W. Halleck, to James A. Hardie, San Francisco, Aug. 1, 1848, *U.S. Gov. Doc. Ser. 573*, pp. 485-86.

101 Halleck, Monterey, to James Alexander Forbes, Santa Clara, Aug. 14, 1847, *ibid.*, p. 595.

important cases. One such special court was appointed on October 30, to try three men accused of kidnapping and murdering Indians.[102] Another special court was convened to hear a case involving counterfeit gold coin. In this particular case Governor Mason, aware of the absence of codified laws for the province, asked the judge to be guided by Mexican law concerning counterfeiting.[103]

Prior to the Treaty of Guadalupe Hidalgo, Colonel Mason almost always insisted on personally appointing the alcaldes. In some rare instances, Mason sanctioned an election, primarily in districts with predominantly American population. For San Francisco he suggested the election of some sort of town legislative body – an *ayuntamiento*.[104] On August 13, 1847, Mason communicated with the First Alcalde of San Francisco, George Hyde, stating:

> There is wanted in San Francisco an efficient town government, more so than is in the power of an alcalde alone to put in force. There may be expected a large number of

---

[102] Mason, Monterey, to J. L. Folsom, San Francisco, Nov. 11, 1847, N. A. Microfilm 82, roll no. 1.

[103] Halleck, Monterey, to J. D. Stevenson, Los Angeles, July 20, 1848, "Archives of California," p. 37.

[104] *The California Star*, San Francisco, Sept. 11, 1847. The *Ayuntamiento* was a popular unit of government in the Spanish colonies. Basically it was a town council composed of alcaldes (justices), regidores (counselors), and a Sindico (city attorney). These officers were generally elected by the town citizens (vecinos). The *Ayuntamiento*, also known in other parts of the Spanish colonies as the cabildo, regulated the towns activities, i.e., licensing of various enterprises, distributing lands to the citizens, providing for local police, maintaining jails and roads and imposing local taxes.

whalers in your bay, and a large increase of your population by the arrival of immigrants. It is therefore highly
necessary that you should at an early day have an efficient
town police, proper town laws; town officers etc., for enforcement of the law; for the preservation of order, for
the proper protection of persons and property.

I therefore desire that you call a town meeting for the
election of such persons who when elected, shall constitute
a town council, and who, in conjunction with the alcalde
shall constitute the town authority until the end of the
year 1848.[105]

The election was held on the sixteenth and William
Glover, William D. M. Howard, William A.
Liedesdorff, E. P. Jones, Robert A. Parker, and
William S. Clark were elected to the council of
San Francisco.[106] A group of laws were then
framed and published regulating licenses, listing
police regulations and fines.[107]

In matters affecting the entire province, Mason
made effective use of the "proclamation" as a
governing device. Soon after his assumption of
office, Governor Mason found it necessary to dis-
courage the desertion of sailors in California by
decreeing stiff sentences to people enticing, con-
cealing or assisting desertion.[108] The problem of
civil marriages was also handled by formal decree.
This, obviously, was a touchy matter in California
with its large Roman Catholic population. Aware
of the dogma of the Roman Catholic Church and

---

105 *Californian,* San Francisco, Sept. 8, 1847.

106 *The California Star,* San Francisco, Sept. 18, 1847.

107 *Laws of the Town of San Francisco, 1847.*

108 Proclamation, Mason, Monterey, Sept. 2, 1847, "Archives of
California."

not wishing to interfere in religious matters, Mason decreed as follows:

> I therefore direct that during the existing state of affairs that no alcalde or other civil officer will perform a marriage ceremony in any case where either of the parties are members of the Catholic Church in California.[109]

In matters of divorce, however, Mason could offer nothing more than some good advice. In a letter to Mrs. Hedy C. Brown of San Francisco he stated:

> Neither he nor any alcalde possess any authority to grant a divorce. If your husband has abandoned you and left the country with no intention of returning and without providing you with any means of resources whatever, I am of the opinion there being no law in California that I can find or hear of on the subject of divorces that he should be viewed as though he was dead as far as you are concerned.[110]

To help him with the increasing duties of military government in California, Colonel Mason appointed First Lieutenant William T. Sherman as Assistant Adjutant General and Lieutenant H. W. Halleck as Secretary of State in California. Basically all legal and land matters were turned over to Lt. Halleck, whose knowledge of Spanish and international law served him well.[111]

---

[109] Circular, Mason, Aug. 23, 1847, "California Military Government Collection, 1846-1849," Bancroft Library.

[110] Mason, Monterey, to Mrs. Hedy C. Brown, San Francisco, Dec. 8, 1847, "Archives of California."

[111] Halleck continued as Secretary of State under General Riley and was also a delegate to the Constitutional Convention. In 1862 Halleck's study on international law was published. It remains authoritative.

When Mason was installed as Governor of California he also assumed the duties and responsibilities of commander in chief of the military forces in the province. In this capacity he ordered all military commanders to lend assistance to civil officers.[112] Military personnel, however, were not subject to civil law, but military law. For the most part the military commanders operated harmoniously with the alcaldes and other civil authorities, but there were some areas of discontent. At Santa Barbara, for example, Captain Francis J. Lippett, the military commander, opposed the alcalde's decision and prevented him from executing it. Mason favored the alcalde and ordered Lippett to desist.[113] Colonel Stevenson in Los Angeles took exception to the alcalde's decision and commuted the fine and sentence of a woman who was convicted of selling liquor to the Indians. Again Mason supported the alcalde and ordered Stevenson to let the law take its course.[114]

A somewhat ludicrous situation occurred in Santa Barbara on April 5, 1848, when a gun belonging to the brig "Elizabeth" was reported missing. Fearing that this gun had fallen into the hands of revolutionaries, a careful search was made, but the gun remained unfound. At length

---

[112] W. T. Sherman, Monterey, to the Alcaldes of San Francisco, Monterey, Santa Barbara, Los Angeles, and San Diego, July 3, 1847, N. A. Microfilm 82, roll no. 1.

[113] Sherman, Monterey, to F. J. Lippett, Santa Barbara, Aug. 25, 1847, *U.S. Gov. Doc. Ser. 573,* pp. 351-2.

[114] Mason, Monterey, to J. D. Stevenson, Los Angeles, June 11, 1848, *ibid.,* pp. 563-64.

Governor Mason levied an assessment on the inhabitants because of the loss of the gun. In informing the military commandant of the southern district, Colonel Stevenson, of Mason's order, W. T. Sherman stated:

> This is the first contribution ever imposed in California, and will require much prudence and care in its collection. All citizens in California, native or naturalized, must pay their respective shares; for it is impossible, under the law of nations, to favor those foreigners who by long residence are so identified with the country that their interests cannot be separated.
>
> Colonel Mason says that you may exempt from the effects of this tax such Americans as, during the late revolution, contributed aid to the American arms and cause.[115]

The gun remained hidden and was found some ten years later. On April 30, 1849, the five hundred dollars and fifty cents that was collected by the military was returned to Santa Barbara by Governor Riley to be used for the purchase or erection of a jail in the city. The inhabitants, however, considered this more humorous than serious and named the streets of Quinientos and El Canon Perdido to commemorate it. Also the former seal of the city of Santa Barbara had a picture of a cannon with the words *vale quinientos pesos.*[116]

---

[115] Sherman, Monterey, to Stevenson, Los Angeles, May 31, 1848, N. A. Microfilm 82, roll no. 1.

[116] Halleck, Monterey, to Don Raymundo Carrillo, Santa Barbara, April 30, 1849, *U.S. Gov. Doc. Ser. 573,* p. 754; William H. Ellison (ed.), "Recollections of William A. Streeter, 1843-1878," *C.H.S.Q.,* XVIII, p. 165.

In matters of foreign trade, Colonel Mason took considerable liberty with official instructions, with the full concurrence of the naval commander Commodore Shubrick. On October 3, 1847, Mason received tariff regulations from Washington which imposed rather severe duties on imports. Realizing the serious complications that would befall California commerce, Mason reduced the port duties and charged from one dollar to fifteen cents a ton and modified the ad valorum charges.[117] On the other hand, he did follow official instructions by replacing all civilian customs collectors with military personnel. In the absence of the naval commander, Mason issued twenty-one custom-house regulations on July 26, 1848, which defined offences and imposed penalties.[118]

The problems of financing the military government in California were neatly solved by Colonel Mason who provided that monies collected from custom duties should be placed in a separate fund. This "Civil Fund," as it was called, was used to defray expenses of government and was controled by the military governor personally.[119] The fund grew very rapidly, especially after the discovery of gold, and soon a considerable surplus accumulated. During the period of military government almost one and one-half million dollars were col-

---

[117] Circular, Mason, Oct. 14, 1847, N. A. Microfilm 82, roll no. 1.

[118] *Ibid.* Custom-house and Port Regulations for the Harbors of California, Mason, July 26, 1848.

[119] B. Riley, Monterey, to J. Hooker, Washington, Aug. 30, 1849, *U.S. Gov. Doc. Ser. 573,* pp. 815-19.

lected, of which almost one million were lent to army and navy in California.[120] After paying rather liberal expenses of the Constitutional Convention in 1849, the "Civil Fund" was turned over to the United States Treasury.[121]

The discovery of gold in California by James Wilson Marshall on January 24, 1848, complicated administration of government. Although the full impact of the discovery was not felt until the following year, army desertions increased alarmingly by July, 1848. As more and more people flocked to the gold fields, Colonel Mason became apprehensive over the absence of law in the mining areas. Fortunately, in February he had invalidated the Mexican system of denouncing claims, thereby preventing a few people from filing on the best mining areas.[122]

On June 12, Mason began his inspection of the gold fields and then reported his findings to Washington. Included in his report were several suggestions concerning the licensing of miners, which were never adopted by the federal government. Once his report was made public the gold rush of 1849 was triggered.[123]

The absence of codified law in California, ex-

---

[120] George W. Crawford, Washington, to L. Taylor, Washington, June 26, 1850, *U.S. Gov. Doc. Ser. 578,* pp. 1-3.

[121] Riley, Monterey, to R. Jones, Washington, Oct. 31, 1849, *U.S. Gov. Doc. Ser. 573,* pp. 850-51.

[122] Proclamation, Mason, Monterey, Feb. 12, 1848, N. A. Microfilm 82, roll no. 1.

[123] Mason, Monterey, to R. Jones, Washington, Aug. 17, 1848, *U.S. Gov. Doc. Ser. 573,* pp. 528-36.

cept for the Mexican law which was unavailable and misunderstood, was a sore point to many people who felt they were completely at the mercy of the alcaldes.[124] Some crimes, involving military personnel, had been defined by official instruction and assigned to military courts. The bulk of the people were unaffected by this and merely wanted to know what the local laws were. Realizing the increasing need for codified laws, Mason proposed a code in May 1848, but wholesale exodus from San Francisco for the mine fields prevented its publication. It was finally published by Sam Brannan of the *California Star* but, unfortunately, was never put in force.[125]

The Treaty of Guadalupe Hidalgo, which was announced in California on August 7, 1848, greatly changed the status of the province and invalidated Mason's laws. As an official part of the United States, California was automatically extended rights under the Constitution and the political laws of the country.[126] Local law, however, had to await Congressional action as regards civil government. Despite some vocal opposition seriously questioning his authority, Colonel Mason continued the military government in force, and he and the people awaited the decision of Congress.[127]

---

[124] *Californian,* San Francisco, Feb. 13, 1848.
[125] *Laws for the Better Government of California* . . . 1848.
[126] See above, p. 22.
[127] *U.S. Const.,* Art. IV, sec. 3, cl. 2.

in the exercise of their functions as heretofore, and when vacancies exist or may occur, they will be filled by regular elections held by the people of several towns and districts, due notice of such elections being previously given. The existing laws of the country will necessarily continue in force until others are made to supply their place. From this new order of things will result to California a new destiny.[3]

The "new order of things" as regards governmental structure, however, was long in coming. Congress, which was the only source of an organic act providing a territorial government for any newly acquired possession, was hopelessly divided on the slavery issue and, at first, even failed to extend the revenue laws to California.[4] These laws, however, automatically became effective in the province upon annexation.

After the treaty was proclaimed in California, the people vociferously demanded civil government. By way of placating them, Colonel Mason's successor, General Bennet Riley, professed to be a civil governor, when in reality he was a military officer in charge of military government.[5] Even Mason proclaimed that civil officers would be elected in the different municipalities of California, but the fact remains that he as well as his successor continued to appoint and direct various

---

[3] *Ibid.*

[4] *The California Star,* San Francisco, Dec. 16, 1848; *Californian,* San Francisco, Nov. 4, 1848.

[5] Proclamation, Riley, Monterey, June 3, 1849, *U.S. Gov. Doc. Ser. 573,* pp. 779-80.

civil officials.[6] In reality, therefore, the government during this period was not appreciably changed. On the other hand, the military governors did not have the same freedom of movement as before and they complained of their confused position. In a letter to General R. Jones, the Adjutant-General in Washington, D.C., Governor Mason outlined his strange situation:

> The above are the only instructions I have received from the department to guide me in the course to be pursued, now that war has ceased, and the country forms an integral part of the United States. For the past two years no civil government has existed here, except that controlled by the senior military or naval officer; and no other officers exist in the country, save the alcaldes confirmed or appointed by myself. To throw off upon them or the people at large the civil management and control of the country, would most probably lead to endless confusion, if not to absolute anarchy; and yet what right or authority have I to exercise civil authority or control in a time of peace in a territory of the United States? Or, if sedition and rebellion should arise, where is my force to meet it?[7]

Mason further stated that although he had no authority and no instructions from the government at Washington to continue the government in California, he would do so rather than place the country in a state of anarchy and confusion by his withdrawal.

The optimistic attitude taken by Governor

---

[6] Mason, Monterey, to J. S. Moerenhout, Monterey, Mar. 19, 1849, *ibid.*, p. 699.

[7] Mason, Monterey, to R. Jones, Washington, Aug. 19, 1848, N. A. Microfilm 82, roll no. 1.

Mason in his proclamation regarding the establishment of civil government by the Congress greatly influenced the attitude of the people. As soon as the Treaty of Guadalupe Hidalgo was announced and California declared to be a part of the United States, the people immediately expected civil government to be proclaimed. They looked hopefully for the arrival of the sloop "St. Mary's" which they thought would bring in the news that Congress had provided an organic law for the territory.[8]

In November a conference took place between Commodore Thomas ap C. Jones, commander of the naval squadron in California and Governor Mason. The results of this meeting as reported by the *California Star* were favorable to civil government. The *Star* reported:

> The growing demand for a judicial organization and the non arrival of the conveyance by which government dispatches and instructions, relative to territorial matters, might have been expected, through long since due, have impressed our authorities, we are most thankful in stating, with the necessity for IMMEDIATE ACTION, and unless the arrival of the "St. Mary's," sloop of war, with the long expected territorial government, shortly occurs, both Com. Jones and Gov. Mason UNITE IN RECOMMENDING THE APPOINTMENT OF A DELEGATE BY THE PEOPLE, TO FRAME LAWS, and make other necessary arrangements for a PROVISIONAL GOVERNMENT for California.[9]

The sloop "St. Mary's" finally arrived bearing

---

[8] *The California Star,* San Francisco, Nov. 26, 1848.
[9] *Ibid.*

the distressing news that Congress had adjourned
without establishing an organic act for California.[10] There arrived instead a long, technical
open letter to the people of California by Secretary
of State James Buchanan. He congratulated the
people of California as citizens of the newly annexed province to the United States and alluded
to the blessings to be gained under the Constitution. After the "window trimming" Buchanan
stated that the President regretted deeply that
Congress did not establish a territorial form of
government during its late session. The letter
closed with the assurance that Congress would at
its next session provide a territorial government
for California. The military government thus continued.[11]

The gold discovery, however, made maintenance
of military government more essential, particularly
as the excitement increased. Entire cities were
almost depopulated as the people flocked to the
gold fields. The expectation of daily earnings many
times their low government salaries caused hun-
dreds of soldiers and sailors to desert and go to
the gold fields. This situation greatly weakened
the military strength in California. Colonel Mason
reported:

> Two companies of regulars, every day diminishing by
> desertions, that cannot be prevented, will soon be the only
> military force in California; and they will be of necessity

10 *Ibid.,* Dec. 16, 1848.
11 Buchanan, Washington, to William V. Vorhies, Washington, Oct.
7, 1848, *U.S. Gov. Doc. Ser. 573,* pp. 6-9.

compelled to remain in San Francisco and Monterey, to
guard the large deposits of powder and munitions of war,
which cannot be removed. . . Since the discovery of
these rich deposits the pay of the troops sent to the country
should be sufficient to prevent their deserting; for, so sure
as men come here at seven dollars a month, they will
desert, with the almost absolute certainty of being able to
make ten or twenty dollars a day in the mines.[12]

In July of 1848, Commodore Jones warned
the Secretary of the Navy of the alarming increase
in desertion. He stated that the safety of the province was gravely threatened. Regarding his command, Jones reported the only positive way to
prevent desertion was to cruise off the coast of
California and, thereby, afford little opportunity
for the men to get ashore and desert.[13]

The military force was further reduced by the
establishment of peace. Volunteer troops who
constituted the bulk of the military units were now
entitled to be mustered out of the service. Many
areas, therefore, were left unprotected. Colonel
Stevenson, at Los Angeles, was informed that "the
pueblo of Los Angeles [was] of necessity aban-
doned," for all available men were needed at
Monterey and San Francisco.[14] A few weeks later
Lieutenant Sherman outlined Mason's seemingly
hopeless situation:

---

[12] Mason, Monterey, to R. Jones, Washington, Aug. 19, 1848, N. A.
Microfilm 82, roll no. 1.

[13] Thomas ap C. Jones, Monterey, to John Y. Mason, Washington,
July 28, 1848, *U.S. Gov. Doc. Ser. 537,* p. 67.

[14] Sherman, Monterey, to J. D. Stevenson, Los Angeles, Aug. 9,
1848, "Stevenson Collection."

> Colonel Mason is in a tight place. In San Francisco there is great disfavor and loud call for assistance. In Los Angeles the same. . . I think the administration have placed Col. Mason in a tight place that might have been avoided. They knew all along that California was not to be given up, and that the population was of a mixed kind, calling for the presence of military force to back the civil authority — that upon the conclusion of the war the volunteers of necessity would be discharged, and that only two companies of regulars would remain. All this they knew at Washington, and yet they have not provided for it.[15]

In Los Angeles Colonel Stevenson recruited citizens into a militia, and then urgently requested Governor Mason to send reinforcements in to protect the city from attack.[16] Other cities were similarly threatened;[17] but, fortunately, no attacks took place. Much as the military was sometimes loathed for its arbitrary methods, the sudden reduction of military power in California caused anxiety on the part of many citizens who felt they were now at the mercy of Indians, brigands and cutthroats. Despite his diminishing forces, Mason hoped to continue administering the government until replacements arrived. He stated:

---

[15] *Ibid.,* Aug. 26, 1848.

[16] *Memorial and Petition of Col. J. D. Stevenson of California,* p. 29. The impression gained from the dispatch is that the withdrawal of military forces had made the city vulnerable to attack by Indians, renegades or bandits.

[17] Captain Folsom presented an ominous picture of the situation in San Francisco. He said; "Acts of disgraceful violence occur almost daily on the shipping and we have no power to preserve order. Tomorrow morning the Volunteers will be mustered out of service, and we shall be utterly without resource for the protection of public property." *U.S. Gov. Doc. Ser. 573,* p. 613.

> Yet, unsustained by military force, or by any positive instructions, I feel compelled to exercise control over the alcaldes appointed, and to maintain order, if possible, in the country, until a civil governor arrive, armed with instructions and laws to guide his footsteps.[18]

Colonel Mason remained and even prepared his own meals when his cook deserted. Yet, happily, there were no serious uprisings to test the effectiveness of the meager military forces under his command.

The establishment of peace and the consequent annexation of California greatly altered the tariff regulations. Heretofore, military officers had been appointed as collectors,[19] but when California was annexed the customs laws of the United States immediately applied. Accordingly Mason ordered the United States tariff of 1846 in force in California. Furthermore, since the revenue collected had to be in a uniform currency, he ordered the collectors not to receive gold dust as payment for duties.[20] The treatment of vessels owned by Californians also presented a problem. Knowing he could not register any vessel, Colonel Mason decided to accept applications of registry from the California owners and forward them to Washington. In the interim, however, in order to prevent hardships by stoppage of trade, Mason granted to

[18] Mason, Monterey, to R. Jones, Washington, Aug. 19, 1848, N. A. Microfilm 82, roll no. 1.

[19] Mason, Monterey, to T. H. Green, Monterey, Oct. 15, 1847, *U.S. Gov. Doc. Ser. 573*, p. 507.

[20] Halleck, Monterey, to J. L. Folsom, San Francisco, Aug. 9, 1848, N. A. Microfilm 82, roll no. 1.

certain ships licenses that enabled them to fly the American flag and trade under its protection.[21]

By December 1848, some attempt was made to put the collection of the revenue back into civil hands. Several civilian collectors were appointed, but military officers were required to have "general supervision of accounts of the collector in order to check any extravagant expenditures or improper use of public money." [22]

Instructions from the Secretary of the Treasury Robert J. Walker were received in California on February 24, 1849. These instructions stated that the annexation of California to the Republic was complete and the Constitution of the United States had therefore been "extended over the entire territory in full force throughout its entire limits." Congress, he said, had not brought the territory within the limits of any collection district nor had it authorized the appointment of any collectors. He realized for this reason that it might be impossible to collect the revenue. Nonetheless, he stated, in all cases of foreign dutiable goods arriving in California and shipped to other places in the United States duties should be collected.[23]

Once again unrealistic tariff instructions from Washington forced Colonel Mason to adopt a separate policy. Mason's Secretary of State, H. W.

[21] *Ibid.*, Halleck, Monterey, to E. H. Harrison, San Francisco, Sept. 25, 1848.

[22] *Ibid.*, Halleck, Monterey, to J. L. Folsom, San Francisco, Sept. 25, 1848.

[23] To Collectors and Other Officers of the Customs, R. J. Walker. Washington, Oct. 7, 1848, *U.S. Gov. Doc. Ser. 573*, p. 45.

Halleck, announced Walker's view, but cogently pointed out the serious weakness. Since there were no collection districts established by Congress in California, he said, no foreign dutiable goods could be introduced. Ships that carried these goods were, therefore, forced to enter some other regular port of the United States and pay the duties prescribed by law. Furthermore, these goods would then have to be transferred to American ships before they could legally be brought into California. The inconvenience and expense resulting from this policy, he stated, have caused the authorities in California to offer the following alternative:

> To pay here all duties and fees, and to execute all papers prescribed by the revenue laws of the United States; and upon their doing so, their goods will be admitted. But, without the execution of such papers, and the payment of such duties and fees, they cannot be allowed to enter or land their cargo; and any attempt to avoid it in this Territory foreign dutiable goods, without the payment of duties, will subject them to all penalties of the law – both vessels and goods will be seized and sent for adjudication in the United States court established in Oregon.[24]

A unanimity of opinion in matters of revenue between the naval and military commanders in California was almost a necessity for the proper operation of customs and duties. Since the naval commander in California, Commodore Thomas ap C. Jones, also supported Mason's alternative it was adopted in all parts of California.[25]

---

[24] Halleck, Monterey, to E. H. Harrison, San Francisco, Feb. 24, 1849, *U.S. Gov. Doc. Ser. 537*, pp. 694-95.

[25] *Ibid.*

Congress on March 3, 1849, created a collection district in San Francisco and assigned a civilian collector, J. C. Collier, to assume control. Collier, however, did not completely take over the responsibilities of office until November 13 of that year.[26] The collection of the revenue in the meantime in California was in mixed civilian-military control (civilian collectors and military inspectors). To all intents and purposes, therefore, military control of collections continued almost down to the time that the military relinquished its authority to elected civil government in California.

When Congress failed to provide an organic act for California the proposals of Commodore Jones and Governor Mason recommending that the people appoint delegates and frame laws for provisional government were taken seriously by the people.[27] Colonel Mason, in view of Secretary Buchanan's letter, deemed it prudent not to create any more excitement regarding civil government and, therefore, remained silent. On December 11, 1849, however, a rather spirited meeting of the citizens of the Pueblo of San Jose took place, demanding provisional civil government.[28] Similar meetings were held in San Francisco, Sacramento, Monterey and Sonoma about the same time.[29] San

[26] W. M. Meredith, Washington, to James Collier, Washington, April 3, 1849; Collier, San Francisco, to W. M. Meredith, Washington, Nov. 13, 1849, *U.S. Gov. Doc. Ser. 573*, pp. 12-15, 24-28.

[27] *The California Star and Californian*, San Francisco, Nov. 26, 1848.

[28] *Ibid.*, Dec. 23, 1848.

[29] *Alta California*, San Francisco, Jan. 4, 25, 1848.

Jose at this time proposed that a general convention be held on the second Monday in January, 1849, at Monterey for the establishment of a provisional government and the nomination of a civil governor and called for delegates from all pueblos in California. At the larger and more important San Francisco meeting on December 11 similar resolutions concerning the establishment of provisional civil government in California were adopted; the date, however, of the projected general convention was changed to March 5, 1849.[30] Delegates for the convention were soon chosen from the largest cities in the north and the success of the movement seemed assured. After several postponements, however, it was decided to await the action of the new Congress regarding territorial status for California.[31] Sectional interest and the lack of a central organization made these meetings nothing more than abortive attempts at popular control of government in California.

A considerable increase in population as a result of the gold discovery was clearly evident, in the last months of 1848. Thousands of miners were working in the gold fields; yet they represented only a small portion of what was yet to come in 1849. The various camps that resulted from the groupings of the miners in the more profitable "diggings" became virtually self-governing units, with few if any ties with the military government in California. Beyond the inspecting of the mine

---

[30] *The California Star and Californian,* San Francisco, Dec. 23, 1848.
[31] *Alta California,* Jan. 24, 1849.

fields and the invalidating of the Mexican system of denouncing mining claims, Colonel Mason did not interfere with mining camps or their government.[32] These mining communities, which later grew into cities, were first governed by rules drawn up in an open meeting. Any serious violation of these rules and a meeting of the citizens was held, a presiding officer and judge elected, a jury of six or twelve persons empaneled, and a trial was held. As these communities increased in importance and population, alcaldes were elected as the chief magistrates.[33] The alcaldes of the mining districts received their authority from the community, and there is no evidence that control by the *de facto* military government in California was ever exercised over them. The remoteness of the mining camps, plus the fear of motivating soldiers to desert, forced the military authorities to remain in the coastal areas of California, thus giving virtual independence to the mining regions.[34]

As early as November of 1848 the duties of military governor began to weigh heavily on the shoulders of Colonel Mason. Complicated with the discovery of gold and the signing of the Treaty of Guadalupe Hidalgo, military government in California was not easily administered. Colonel Mason, therefore, despairing of his position, requested to be relieved of his command. In a letter

[32] M'Collum, *California As I Saw It*, p. 51.
[33] Root, *Journal of Travels*, pp. 129-31.
[34] M'Collum, *op. cit.*, p. 52.

to the Adjutant-General in Washington, Mason
stated:

> The war being over, the soldiers nearly all deserted, and
> having now been from the states two years, I respectfully
> request to be ordered home. I feel the less hesitancy in
> making this request, as it is the second only that I recollect
> ever to have made, in more than thirty years service, to be
> relieved from duty upon which I have been placed: the
> first was asking to be relieved from the recruiting service,
> in 1832, that I might join my company in the Black Hawk
> war.[35]

His request was granted, but five months passed
before he was officially relieved.

On February 28, 1849, Brevet Major General
Persifor F. Smith arrived in San Francisco and
assumed the military command of the Third Division (Pacific Division).[36] This was comprised
of the Tenth Military Department which included
California and the Eleventh Military Department,
which was the Oregon Territory. The War Department had combined the two departments in a
military geographical division thus strengthening
the military command on the Pacific Coast.[37] The
combined departments were able, if necessary, to
put a larger and more formidable force in the
field. Each military department, however, retained

---

[35] Mason, Monterey, to R. Jones, Washington, Nov. 24, 1848, *U.S.
Gov. Doc. Ser. 573,* p. 649.

[36] Persifor F. Smith, San Francisco, to R. Jones, Washington, Mar.
15, 1849, *ibid.,* pp. 711-13.

[37] W. L. Marcy, Washington, to Persifor F. Smith, Nov. 15, 1848.
U.S. Gov. Doc. Ser. 573, p. 649.

its own commanding officer, the one in California at the time being Colonel Mason. Although senior in rank, General Smith did not interfere with the administration of California and appears to have had only the authority of co-ordinating the troops of both departments in joint military operations.[38]

Some authorities, however, erroneously claim that he succeeded Colonel Mason as military governor. But the record shows that although there were people who considered General Smith as supreme in California and sent him letters requesting favors and making reports, General Smith always forwarded the correspondence to the proper military governor, Colonel Mason.[39]

Some trepidation was felt by Colonel Mason as he continued to administer the military government in the early months of 1849. This was evidenced by the noticeable reduction of instructions to the local officers and the "hands off" policy assumed by Mason regarding various meetings for the establishment of provisional civil government.[40] One of Mason's last pronouncements as governor of California is of some importance since it defines the legal status of the Indian and his right of self-government. Mason stated:

---

[38] Marcy, Washington, to Bennet Riley, New York, Oct. 10, 1848, *ibid.*, pp. 260-61.

[39] Mason, San Francisco, to M. Scott, Jr., April 9, 1849, *ibid.*, page 703.

[40] Halleck, Monterey, to Alex Perry, San Francisco, Jan. 2, 1849, *ibid.*, p. 687.

council, nor the council elected on January 15, 1849. Complicating matters was also the mass meeting held in Portsmouth Square on February 12, 1849, where the constitution and laws for the city of San Francisco, "not repugnant to the Constitution of the United States and common law," were passed. A legislative body of fifteen members was established called the "Legislative Assembly of the District of San Francisco" which was to assume its duties on the first Monday of March. At the same time three justices of the peace were appointed and were vested with civil and criminal jurisdiction. The Assembly also appointed a committee to take up their cause with General Smith and Commodore Jones, the senior military and naval officers in California.[46]

General Smith, in supporting military government, issued his statement that the legislative committee was in violation of the authority in Washington and that the present *de facto* government could only be superseded by action of the Congress of the United States. He also threatened to arrest, remove and punish any civil officer clearly violating the laws of the United States.[47]

Governor Mason, during whose term of office

---

[46] James Findla, *Statement of a Few Events,* MS in Bancroft Library, p. 10; Francis J. Lippett, *Reminiscences,* p. 77; James Creighton, George Hyde, Henry A. Harrison, Thomas J. Roach, Talbot H. Green, San Francisco, to P. G. Smith, San Francisco, Mar. 20, 1849, *U.S. Gov. Doc. Ser. 573,* pp. 728-9.

[47] Smith, San Francisco, to James Creighton [et al.], San Francisco, Mar. 27, 1849, *U.S. Gov. Doc. Ser. 573,* pp. 735-38.

these elections and mass meetings occurred, declined to take any official position respecting them. General Riley, who succeeded Mason, suspended the alcalde, Dr. Thaddeus M. Leavenworth, against whom charges of maladministration had been made by the Assembly. The Assembly continued to operate enacting laws, creating and filling new offices and abolishing the office of alcalde and forcibly deposing the alcalde, Dr. Leavenworth.[48] The action of this Assembly caused Riley to issue a proclamation addressed "To the people of the district of San Francisco." He warned the citizens of San Francisco not to recognize the illegal and unauthorized Assembly of San Francisco. He then called upon them to restore order and return all archival records to Alcalde Leavenworth who "was legally constituted" authority of district. He then stated:

> The office of alcalde is one established by law, and all officers of the United States have been ordered by the President to recognize and support the legal authority of the person holding such office; and whatever feelings of prejudice or personal dislike may exist against the individual holding such office, the office itself should be sacred. For any incompetency or maladministration the law affords abundant means of remedy and punishment – means which the executive will always be found ready and willing to employ to the full extent of the powers in him vested.[49]

[48] Riley, Monterey, J. [sic] M. Leavenworth, San Francisco, May 6, 1849, *ibid.*, p. 760; Ryan, *Personal Adventures,* p. 78.

[49] Proclamation to the District of San Francisco, Riley, Monterey, June 4, 1849, *U.S. Gov. Doc. Ser. 573,* pp. 773-74.

On the following day, June 5, Governor Riley accepted the resignation of Dr. Leavenworth as alcalde and appointed a committee to supervise a special election for the vacancy.[50]

The arrival of the United States steamer "Edith" on June 1 with news that Congress had adjourned without organizing a territorial government for California, forced General Riley's hand. Two days later, on June 3, he issued a proclamation in which he defined the legal status of California and called for a Constitutional Convention. His position in California, he explained, was that of "an executive of the existing civil government." This was a curious statement and one not easily understood. The General had succeeded a military governor, Colonel Mason, and continued in virtually the same administrative patterns of his predecessor – appointing and supervising municipal officials. Yet he considered this civil government.[51] He further stated:

> The undersigned, in accordance with instructions from the Secretary of War has assumed the administration of civil affairs in California not as a military governor, but as an executive of the existing civil government. In the absence of a properly appointed civil governor, the commanding officer of the department is, by the laws of California, ex officio civil governor of the country; and the

[50] Riley, Monterey, to R. A. Parker, Frederick Billings, John Servine, W. S. Clark, Stephen Harris, B. R. Buckalew, William H. Tillinghurst, A. J. Grayson and J. P. Haven, San Francisco, June 5, 1849, *ibid.*, pp. 775-76.

[51] Proclamation, Riley, June 3, 1849, *ibid.*, pp. 776-80.

instructions from Washington were based on the provisions
of these laws. This subject had been misrepresented, or at
least misconceived, and currency given to the impression that the government of the country is still military.
Such is not the fact. The military government ended with
the war, and what remains is a civil government recognized
in the existing laws of California.[52]

He pointed out that no military officer other than
himself could exercise any civil authority by virtue
of the military commission. As commanding general of the department he served as ex officio
officer of the civil government. The laws of California existing before the conquest, and not inconsistent with the laws, constitution and treaties of
the United States were still in force and would
continue until changed by some competent authority.

General Riley then addressed the proponents
for provisional civil government by stating that
the situation in California was different from that
in Oregon, in that the former had a system of laws
which, with some changes and amendments, should
continue until repealed by Congress. Comparing
the situation in California as being identical with
that of Louisiana in 1803, he referred to Supreme
Court decisions recognizing the validity of laws
existing in that province previous to annexation.
He warned the citizens that they should accept
this fact and, therefore, not put their faith in laws
which would not be recognized by the legitimate

[52] *Ibid.*

courts of the land. Placating the proponents of
civil government by calling a convention to "frame
a constitution or territorial organization for the
province," Riley appealed to their sense of order
by asking support of the "existing government."
He stated:

> As Congress has failed to organize a new territorial
> government, it becomes our imperative duty to take some
> active means to provide for the existing wants of the coun-
> try. This, it is thought, may be best accomplished by put-
> ting in full vigor the administration of the laws as they
> now exist, and completing the organization of the civil
> government by the election and appointment of all officers
> recognized by law; while at the same time a convention in
> which all parts of the territory are represented, shall meet
> and frame a state constitution, or territorial organization
> to be submitted to the people for their ratification, and then
> proposed to Congress for its approval. Considerable time
> will necessarily elapse before any new government can be
> legitimately organized and put in operation; in the interim,
> the existing government, if its organization be completed,
> will be found sufficient for all our temporary wants.[53]

General Riley's action in calling a constitutional
convention was completely extra-legal, for he had
no authority to do so. He stated, however, in his
proclamation that this course was advised by the
President and the Secretaries of State and War,
but an examination of orders from Washington
does not bear him out. The advisability of calling
such a convention had been urgently recommended

---

[53] *Ibid.*

by his predecessor, Colonel Mason;[54] but this in itself did not constitute proper authority. The only justification, therefore, lay with the "laws of necessity" under an administration of military government. But General Riley claimed he was civil governor and that military government had ceased. The political unrest existing in California which resulted in several serious attempts to establish a provisional government, doubtless prompted General Riley to assume leadership of a movement to frame a state constitution or territorial organization. By doing so he "stole the thunder" from the proponents of civil government, retained his authority and prestige as *de facto* governor of California and, far more important, was able to lend unity and organization to such a movement. Furthermore, by calling the convention General Riley was able to keep a closer watch over the proceedings and exert some influence in stemming any wild schemes.[55]

In his proclamation of June 3 Governor Riley listed the various departments of the *de facto* government of California. The executive power, he stated, was vested in a governor who was appointed by the supreme government (the United States). In the event that such an appointment was not made, the commanding military officer of the

---

[54] *Ibid.*, Riley, Monterey, to R. Jones, Washington, June 30, 1849, pp. 748-52.

[55] The insinuations raised that the convention was influenced by General Riley were vehemently denied by the first Senators and Representatives. Memorial. . . *U.S. Gov. Doc. Ser. 581*, p. 14.

department would assume the office. He continued:

> Second, a secretary, whose duties and powers are also properly defined. Third, a territorial or departmental legislature with limited powers to pass laws of a local character. Fourth, a superior court (tribunal superior) of the territory, consisting of four judges and a fiscal. Fifth, a prefect and sub-prefect for each district, who are charged with the preservation of public order and the execution of the laws: their duties correspond, in a great measure with those of district marshals or sheriffs. Sixth, a judge of first instance for each district (this office is, by a custom not inconsistent with the laws, vested in the first alcalde of the district). Seven, alcaldes who have concurrent jurisdiction among themselves in the same district, but are subordinate to the higher judicial tribunals. Eighth, local justices of the peace. Ninth, *ayuntamientos,* or town councils. The powers and functions of all these officers are fully defined in the laws of this country, and are most identical with those of the corresponding offices in the Atlantic and western states.[56]

He then proclaimed the first of August as a day for holding special elections for the delegates to the general convention and for filling the offices of the superior court, prefects, and sub-prefects and vacant alcalde offices. In the election of superior justices, one judge was to be elected from the districts of San Diego, Los Angeles and Santa Barbara; one from San Luis Obispo and Monterey; one from San Jose and San Francisco; and

---

[56] Proclamation, Riley, Monterey, June 3, 1849, *U.S. Gov. Doc. Ser. 573,* pp. 776-80.

one from Sonoma, Sacramento, and San Joaquin. Members of the territorial legislature were to be elected at the annual election in November. Suffrage was extended to all male citizens twenty-one years of age, of the United States and Upper California, resident in California at the time of the election. The proclamation finally concluded with a rather vague boundary definition of the ten districts in California, which included San Diego, Los Angeles, Santa Barbara, San Luis Obispo, Monterey, San Jose, San Francisco, Sonoma, Sacramento, and San Joaquin.[57]

The elections were held on August 1 as scheduled, and municipal officers and delegates selected. Chosen also were the justices of the superior court which included Peter H. Burnett as Chief Justice, and Jose M. Covarrubias, Pacificus Ord and Lewis Dent as Associate Justices. Despite the "official election," the officers chosen assumed office only when duly appointed by the military governor.[58] Although no elected municipal offices were denied appointment by General Riley, the fact that he officially installed them in office indicates the power of the military commander who styled himself as *de facto* civil governor.

Once the various officials were installed the government began to function under the slightly altered Mexican laws of 1837. General Riley was

---

[57] *Ibid.*

[58] Riley, Monterey, to Peter H. Burnett, Aug. 13, 1849, Burnett, *Recollections and Opinions of an Old Pioneer*, p. 346.

relieved of the responsibility of reviewing cases of
the lower courts of the alcaldes which now went by
direct appeal to the superior tribunal.[59]

In September the Mexican laws of March 20
and May 23, 1837, translated by H. W. Halleck
and W. E. P. Hartnell, were printed by the *Alta
California*. This compilation of laws entitled
*Translation and Digest of Such Portions of the
Mexican Laws of March 20 and May 23, 1837 As
Are Supposed To Be Still In Force and Adopted
to the Present Condition of California With Introduction and Notes,* was made available to the
different judicial officers in California, specifically
charging them to use these laws as a basis for their
decisions.[60]

Despite codified laws and elected officers, the
modified Mexican plan of government was repugnant to the Americans. The broad powers of the
alcaldes and prefects were no less odious in the
hands of elected officers. Furthermore, Mexican
laws to them were inferior and therefore unaccept-
able. The bright prospect of state or territorial
government, however, made the "Riley" government somewhat more tolerable.[61] Nonetheless,
grumbling continued even as the convention
worked on a state constitution.

[59] Halleck, Monterey, to J. E. Brackett, Sonoma, Aug. 17, 1849;
Halleck, Monterey, to Juan José Needa, Sept. 4, 1849; *U.S. Gov. Doc.
Ser. 573,* p. 809, 826.

[60] *Alta California,* San Francisco, 1849.

[61] *The Placer Times,* Sacramento, June 26, 1849.

The convention met at Monterey on September 1 and by October 12 had formed a state constitution. A month later its ratification by an almost unanimous vote was announced and it was declared ordained and established. On December 20, 1849, General Bennet Riley yielded his authority to the newly-elected Governor under the Constitution of California, Peter H. Burnett.[62]

[62] Riley, Monterey, to R. Jones, Washington, Oct. 31, 1849; *U.S. Gov. Doc. Ser. 573*, p. 830; Proclamation, Riley, Monterey, Dec. 20, 1849, *U.S. Gov. Doc. Ser. 561*, p. 40.

HENRY W. HALLECK

Served as secretary of state under Governors Mason and Riley. From Heyman's *Prudent Soldier: E. R. S. Canby.*

MAJOR GENERAL BENNET RILEY

As military governor from April to December 1849, Riley called California's Constitutional Convention. Courtesy of the Public Information Office, Fort Riley.

COLONEL RICHARD B. MASON
Served the longest period as military governor, May 1847 to April 1849,
and during his tenure issued the celebrated report on the gold fields.
Courtesy of the Bancroft Library.

Alcalde Rule

Doubtless the most important single officer in the administration of local government in California, both before and after the American conquest, was the alcalde. This magistrate, who was a part of the time-honored governmental system of the Spanish colonies, was an adaptation of the Arabian and Moorish Al-Cadi or village judge.[1] The practice of selecting an alcalde remained in some towns in Spain after the Moors were expelled. Not universally adopted by Spanish towns, the office of alcalde was, nonetheless, sufficiently recognized as an efficient instrument of government to be extended to the colonies of Spain, and included and described in the *Recopilación de Leyes de los Reynos de las Indias,* the governmental structure of all of the Spanish çolonies.

The term alcalde, which has no precise English equivalent, (closely corresponds to judge or justice of the peace) was adopted for various offices in the government of the Spanish çolonies. There were, for example, *alcaldes del crimén, alcaldes de minas,* and *alcaldes ordinarios,* to mention a few. The leading civil magistrate, however, in the colonies of New Spain, where local government

---

[1] The Appendix (1850), Cal. Rep. 559: Edward Lane-Poole, *A Thousand and One Nights,* pp. 168-69, 278-79.

was more or less uniform, was the alcalde ordinario. Early assuming patriarchal characteristics,
the *alcalde ordinario* was considered the father of
the village and was usually elected to office. In the
Laws of the Indies, which were later modified and
supplanted by the Spanish Cortes of 1813 and the
Mexican Congress of 1824, some twenty-five
articles describe and define duties of alcaldes.
Aside from rather perfunctory stipulations, that
alcaldes be honest, literate and capable, the *Laws
of the Indies* also provided that alcaldes be elected
officials.[2]

The introduction of the office of alcalde in California corresponded with the establishment of the
pueblo by Governor Felipe de Neve in 1781. In
his famous *Reglamento para Gobierno de la Provincia de Californias* on October 21, 1781, Governor Neve provided for the appointment of
alcaldes.[3] Title Fourteen on the political government and instruction for settlers states:

> And as is meet for the good and proper government of
> the pueblos, the administration of justice, direction of
> public works, apportionment of water, and careful watch-
> fulness over whatever has been provided in these Instruc-
> tions that the pueblos be given, in proportion to the num-
> ber of inhabitants, ordinary alcaldes and other magistrates
> yearly, these for the first two years shall be appointed by
> the governor and in the following years the settlers shall
> nominate by and from themselves the public officials that

---

[2] *Recopilación de Leyes,* Tomo I, Libro II, Titulo 17; Tomo II, Libro
IV, Titulo 21; Tomo II, Libro V, Titulo 2.

[3] *Reglamento para el Gobierno de la Provincia de Californias,*
Titulo Catorce, Ley 18.

shall have been arranged for. These elections must pass for their confirmation to the Governor by whom said nominations shall be continued if he deems it expedient.[4]

Therefore, the pueblos San Jose, Los Angeles and the Villa de Branciforte (later part of Santa Cruz), were the first communities in California to be granted alcaldes as their civil magistrates.[5]

During the Spanish period in California some rather serious limitations were placed on the alcalde's authority. This limitation was nothing more than the extension of military control over the municipality. Although the citizens of the pueblos were allowed to elect an alcalde and other officers of the *ayuntamiento*, the real authority in the town lay in the governor's appointed military representative called the *comisionado* (commissioner). Generally holding the rank of corporal or sergeant in the army, the *comisionado* was charged with many responsibilities. He conferred upon the citizens full right and title to their lands, kept the peace, collected local taxes, executed the governor's decrees, supervised the public works and guarded the manners and morals of the pueblo. Both alcalde and *ayuntamiento* were subordinate to the *comisionado* who could annul the acts of the town council and the decisions of the magistrate. The practice of appointing a *comisionado* ended with the termination of Spanish control and under the Mexican

---

[4] *Regulation for Governing the Province of the Californias,* translated by John Everett Johnson.

[5] H. W. Halleck, Monterey, to R. B. Mason, Monterey, Mar. 1, 1849, *U.S. Gov. Doc. Ser. 573,* p. 125.

governors in California the alcalde assumed the
position of power in the municipality, although
he could not legally annul the acts of the *ayuntamiento*.[6]

At the time of the United States occupation,
California was being governed under the Mexican
constitution of 1837. Two special acts of that year,
one on March 30 and the other on May 23, reor-
ganized the provincial government in California
and also redefined the qualifications and functions
of the alcalde.[7] Under this new plan the governor
remained the chief executive officer, but new local
districts were established, headed by prefects and
subprefects. The alcalde was thus relegated to a
rather minor role. Characteristically, the complete
and successful execution of these laws did not take
place under the Mexican government.[8] Ironically,
it was the United States military government under
General Bennet Riley in April, 1849, that succeeded
in implementing most of the provisions outlined in
these two acts.[9] Prior to the American occupation,
the instability of government, which in California
was harassed by many revolutions, caused the delay
in executing the laws of 1837.

It was this delay, curiously enough, that gave

---

[6] Donald C. Cutter, "Moraga of the Military: His California Service," pp. 7 *ff.*

[7] J. Halleck [sic] and W. E. P. Hartnell, *Translation and Digest of
Such Portion of the Mexican Laws of March 20th and May 23rd.* . .

[8] *Mena* v. *Le Roy*, 1 Cal. Rep., 216; *Reynolds* v. *West*, 1 Cal. Rep.
322.

[9] Proclamation to the People of California, B. Riley, June 3, 1849,
U.S. Gov. Doc. Ser. 573, pp. 776-80.

the office of alcalde in California added strength.
Since prefects and subprefects were not appointed
in most districts in California, the duties of these
new posts ultimately devolved upon the functioning office of alcalde.[10] On the other hand, however,
according to the laws of 1837, there were only
four towns in California that were legally entitled
to alcaldes. Under the act of March 20, only the
capital of California, coastal towns with a population of four thousand inhabitants, interior towns of
eight thousand inhabitants and towns that had
alcaldes prior to 1808 were granted permission to
elect alcaldes as civil magistrates. The only areas
in California, therefore, legally entitled to alcaldes
were the three towns, Los Angeles, Santa Cruz,
San Jose, and the capital, Monterey, for there
were no communities with a population of four
thousand until some time after the American occupation.[11]

The qualifications for holding the office of alcalde were indeed few. Honesty, ability, and
literacy were basic requirements desired of, and
unhappily rarely found in, all office holders. There
were, however, certain specific qualifications that
an alcalde needed to hold office. In the first place,
he was to be a citizen of the pueblo from which he
was being elected. Secondly, he had to be a civilian,
for no soldier was allowed to hold that office
except in certain rare cases. Thirdly, he was not to
be in debt to the treasury of the province. These

---

10 *Mena* v. *Le Roy,* 1 Cal. Rep. 488.
11 Halleck, *Digest of Mexican Laws,* p. 2.

simple requirements, which were not always carefully observed, made the selection of candidates
for this office anything but a difficult task.[12]

For the most part, alcaldes in California were
elected by the citizens of the town, although Neve's
proclamation expressed some doubt of the early
citizens' ability to govern themselves and provided
for the appointment of these officers for the first
two years.[13] Furthermore, provision was made for
the governor to appoint alcaldes any time it proved
necessary. Appointments of alcaldes, therefore,
were made both in the Spanish and Mexican
periods in California, as indeed they were during
the American occupation.[14]

Clearly the town's most powerful man (especially during the Mexican period) the alcalde
carried his insignia of office on his cane. This
silver-headed cane of the alcalde was a power in
itself. Not only did it represent the office of alcalde
but also it carried the official power along with it.
If for some reason the alcalde could not be present
at an official function, he would send his cane. It
was somewhat surprising to Americans appointed
to the office of alcalde to see the authority of the
cane always being respected. One such American
alcalde commented: "How comforting it is for
one to carry his small power at the end of his
cane!"[15]

[12] *Recopilación de Leyes,* Tomo ii, Libro v, Titulo 3.
[13] *Reglamento,* Titulo Catorce, Ley 14.
[14] *Ibid.;* also see above, p. 107.
[15] Walter Colton, *Three Years in California,* p. 19.

Characteristically, the extent of jurisdiction of alcaldes in California was unclear and ill-defined. Certainly his authority was not confined to the immediate boundaries of a small pueblo. More often it extended far into the surrounding country. The districts served by alcaldes ranged from three to five hundred square miles, usually with no definite boundary except the Pacific Ocean.[16] There were areas where the jurisdiction of alcaldes necessarily overlapped, but this created no serious problem since either alcalde would accept jurisdiction in such cases.[17] In some of the large districts such as Sonoma, which extended from the Bay of San Francisco to the border of Oregon, the alcalde was permitted to appoint auxiliary alcaldes to help him administer the area. Many times these auxiliary alcaldes were appointed from the larger ranchers in the areas. These auxiliary alcaldes usually exercised authority in an indefinite area within their own neighborhood.[18]

Before taking office, each elected alcalde secured the written approval of the governor of the province. Some measure of control was exercised by the governor over the alcaldes, for not only did he review his election to office but he also passed approval on decisions appealed to him. During the American period of military government, especially under the administration of Colonel Rich-

---

[16] Proclamation to the People of California, B. Riley, Monterey, June 3, 1849, *U.S. Gov. Doc. Ser. 573,* pp. 776-80.

[17] *The California Star,* San Francisco, Mar. 20, 1847.

[18] Washington A. Bartlett, San Francisco, to Don Carlos Weber, San Francisco, Oct. 14, 1846, "William Leidesdorff Papers."

ard B. Mason, (1847-1849) the alcaldes were more closely supervised.[19] In the later period of American military government, during the gold rush period, the alcaldes elected in the mining camps were virtually autonomous and received no interference from military governors.[20] It was customary under the Spanish and Mexican governments for the governor to give elaborate instructions in confirming alcaldes. These instructions usually reiterated general responsibilities and greatly idealized duties and authority of alcaldes. The Americans, on the other hand, simply filled in the appropriate blanks on pre-written forms in appointing or confirming appointment of an alcalde. Generally these forms stated:

> Know all men by these presents, that I, Richard B. Mason, Colonel, First Regiment Dragoons, United States Army, and Governor of California, by virtue of the authority in me vested, do hereby appoint —— —— alcalde for and in the town of ——.[21]

The patriarchal aspects of the office of alcalde, in which he was entrusted with judicial, executive and legislative functions of government, were definitely a marked contrast to the American ideas of government, and, therefore, difficult for Americans to understand or accept.[22] The Spanish and Mexican practice of combining the legislative,

---

[19] Halleck, *Digest of Mexican Laws,* p. 9.

[20] William S. McCollum, *California As I Saw It,* p. 43.

[21] Mason, Monterey, to J. D. Stevenson, Los Angeles, June 1, 1847, *U.S. Gov. Doc. Ser. 573,* p. 316.

[22] *The California Star,* San Francisco, Dec. 23, 1848.

judicial and executive functions in one officer had served them well and was an accepted form of government. When the American forces arrived they continued the alcalde in office and it was not uncommon, therefore, even during the period of American military government, for an alcalde to apprehend and arrest a person, preside over his trial, pass judgment and finally execute the sentence.[23] When Walter Colton was appointed alcalde of Monterey by Commodore Stockton, he was awed with the power of the office. He stated:

> [This office] devolves upon me duties similar to those of mayors in one of our cities, without any of those judicial aides which he enjoys. It involves every breach of the peace, every case of crime, every business obligation, and every disputed land title within a space of three hundred miles . . . such an absolute disposal of questions affecting property and personal liberty never ought to be confided to one man. There is not a judge on any bench in England or the United States whose power is so absolute as that of the alcalde of Monterey.[24]

According to the Mexican laws of May 23, 1837, the judicial procedure of alcaldes' courts was defined as three distinct forms. The first was simply conciliation or arbitration. In this trial the parties to the dispute were allowed to bring two arbiters (*hombres buenos*), one selected by each of the litigants. These *hombres buenos* heard the facts in the case, considered the evidence in the law in-

[23] Stephen J. Field, *Personal Reminiscences of Early Days in California*, p. 30.

[24] Colton, *Three Years in California*, p. 55.

volved, and, after a certain period, submitted their opinion to the alcalde, who rendered a decision in the case within eight days. This trial of conciliation was primarily advisory, for once the alcalde rendered his decision it could either be accepted or rejected by the parties in dispute. If the decision was accepted, the alcalde entered a concise account of the trial in his "Book of Conciliations," which was signed by him, the arbiters, and the parties involved. If the parties disagreed with the alcalde's decision, they were merely obligated to pay the cost. The alcalde's decision in this case was, thus, far from binding.[25]

The second form of judicial procedure was referred to as the "verbal process." In this procedure the alcalde could try

> . . . civil complaints which [did] not exceed $100.00, and criminal ones respecting trifling injuries and other similar faults that [did] not merit any other punishment than a slight reprehension or correction.[26]

The plaintiff presented his complaint orally to the alcalde, who then summoned the defendant. Each party to this suit was ordered to bring his arbiter and these *"hombres buenos"* listened carefully to the facts of the case. The alcalde then heard the opinion of the arbiters and within eight days pronounced his "definitive sentence or decision," and this was subsequently executed by the alcalde himself. Again a concise account of the

---

[25] Halleck, *Digest of Mexican Laws,* p. 15.
[26] *Ibid.*

proceedings was entered in the "Book of Verbal Processes" which was signed by the alcalde, the *"hombres buenos,"* the contestants and, in this case, the secretary or clerk. The decision of the alcalde in this case was final, and no appeal was allowed to any other tribunal in the province.[27]

A Court of First Instance provided for under the laws of May 23, 1837, was considered the chief tribunal in the district. Its jurisdiction extended over civil and criminal cases "of whatever description," the exception being cases where military personnel and clergymen were involved. The governor usually appointed the Judge of First Instance, but in the event the appointment was not made, the senior alcalde of the district assumed the post. Before long the first alcalde of the district automatically became the Judge of First Instance.[28]

The judicial procedure of the Court of First Instance was definitely more formal. Written complaints were filed, witnesses called, and a summary of the case made and sent to the plaintiff and defendant, both of whom were given opportunity to reply. Then briefs of both sides were received and made public. After a serious examination of the briefs, the summary and the facts, the alcalde published a verdict in eight days. The verdict was then sent to the governor, and if it was approved, the sentence was carried out by the alcalde.[29]

Various other judicial duties occupied the time

---

[27] *Ibid.*
[28] *Ibid.; Mena* v. *Le Roy,* 1 Cal. Rep. 220.
[29] *Ibid.*

of the alcalde. There were such things as witnessing of signatures, granting of various licenses, appointing guardians to minors, opening of wills and making them public, and appointing executors to estates. Although only one aspect of his total responsibility, the judicial duties of the alcalde consumed most of his time and were of greater service to the district.

The legislative responsibilities of the office of alcalde stemmed from his position as presiding officer of the town council or *ayuntamiento*. The *ayuntamiento,* another feature of town government, was also provided for in the Laws of the Indies. Its introduction in California similarly coincides with Felipe de Neve's *Reglamento* concerning the establishment of the pueblos.[30] Beginning with an alcalde and two *regidores,* the *ayuntamiento* was eventually enlarged to include almost a dozen members. As the presiding officer of the *ayuntamiento,* the alcalde opened and closed the sessions, appointed various committees and often played a strong role in the finances of the pueblo. In regular proceedings of the town council the alcalde had a voice and a vote. The jurisdiction of the *ayuntamiento* was not co-terminous with that of the alcalde and did not extend beyond the physical limits of the pueblo.[31]

The chief legislation of the *ayuntamiento* concerned the welfare of the town and embraced such items as caring for the streets, cemeteries, sanitary

[30] *Ibid.; Reglamento,* Titulo Catorce, Ley 18.
[31] *Recopilación de Leyes,* Tomo II, Libro V, Titulo 12, Ley 17.

affairs, prisons and hospitals of the city; inspecting
provisions, liquors and drugs; recording births,
marriages and deaths; establishing market places,
paved streets, bridges, parks and public fountains.
It also had the power to establish schools, and pay
teachers out of municipal funds. Finally, it was to
watch over the weights and measures, handle
monies honestly and make annual reports to the
governor. As presiding officer the alcalde could
have had a great deal of influence in the *ayuntamiento*.[32] During the American occupation, the
alcalde at San Francisco was greatly disturbed
over his wide authority. He petitioned the governor to divorce the alcalde from the town council,
thereby relieving the alcalde of some duties and
making the town council a more independently
functioning organization. The governor, however,
refused to alter the duties and authority of the
alcaldes.[33]

The executive functions of the alcaldes probably
ranked next in importance to the judicial functions. As the executive officer of his district, he
was charged with executing all the acts of the
ayuntamiento.[34] He was also responsible for enforcing any ordinances and degrees promulgated
by the provincial administration. Typically when
the alcalde received a decree, he notified the inhabitants of the village by beating a drum, and,

[32] Halleck, *Digest of Mexican Laws*, p. 15.

[33] George Hyde, San Francisco, to R. B. Mason, Monterey, Mar. 20,
1848, "Archives of California"; Mason, Monterey, to Hyde, San Francisco, Mar. 27, 1848, *U.S. Gov. Doc. Ser. 573*, p. 500.

[34] Halleck, *Digest of Mexican Laws*, p. 15.

when they were properly assembled, the document was read. The order or proclamation was then posted in some conspicuous public place and became the law. Many of the laws of the governor and even orders from the Mexican congress or president were proclaimed by the alcalde in this manner.[35] The granting of pueblo lands also came under the authority of the alcalde as executive officer. The petitions for pueblo lands were received by the *ayuntamiento* and, generally, referred to a committee which was charged with reviewing these petitions. When the petition was approved, it was turned over to the alcalde, who made the actual grant of land. Each such grant was entered in a book and a copy of the deed was given to the person receiving the land. Unfortunately, however, the legal process, at times was cumbersome, and, therefore, extra-legal land grants were made, the result being that the question of land titles arose and became the most important legal controversy in the early statehood of California.[36]

Charged with securing the good order and welfare of the district, the alcalde was required to reprimand idle, wicked, and vagrant individuals; patrol the streets at night to see that all was orderly; see to it that the citizens of the town lived by useful occupations; and call upon a military force and/or muster the citizens in a military unit for the defense of the town.[37] There also were

---

[35] Alfred Robinson, *Life in California*, pp. 161-64.
[36] *Reynolds* v. *West,* 1 Cal. Rep. 327.
[37] Halleck, *op. cit.,* p. 16.

many privileges for which the alcalde issued licenses, such as the cutting of timber, use of pueblo lands, and the holding of a fandango.[38] He inspected hides brought into the town for market purposes and saw that they were properly branded. Passports needed to enter and leave the town were issued by him and there were even cases where the alcalde taught the village school.[39]

It is no wonder then, in view of the many and varied duties of the alcalde that he was often referred to as the father of the village. Certainly a conscientious person in the office of alcalde would have found it almost impossible to reserve a spare moment for personal affairs.

When the United States forces occupied California in July, 1846, they found the alcalde as the chief local administrative officer. It was expedient for the military commanders of the United States to continue the office of alcalde and to retain as many loyal Californians in the office as was practicable.[40] The combination of legislative executive and judicial duties in one man, although odious to many American immigrants in California, was nevertheless advantageous to the military governors in California. The conflicts that would necessarily arise with the division of these functions in separate individuals was prevented by the

---

[38] A Spanish or Spanish-American ball or dance at which the dance "fandango" may be performed. A man and a woman both with castanets dance the "fandango," the music being played in triple time.

[39] Josiah Belden, "Statement of Historical Facts of California," p. 32. MS in Bancroft Library.

[40] Proclamation, July 7, 1846, John D. Sloat, U.S. Gov. Doc. Ser. 493, pp. 664-65.

adoption of the alcalde system by the Americans.

The proclamation issued by Commodore Sloat July 7, 1846, called upon the alcaldes and "other civil officers" to retain their offices and continue their functions as before. There were, however, alcaldes whose loyalty would not permit them to function under American military rule, and in these cases Commodore Sloat appointed Americans, usually naval officers, to replace them. The appointment of American alcaldes was generally made by the military governor, although there is evidence that subordinate military commanders made alcalde appointments. For example, Captain John Montgomery, the military commander of the northern sector of California including the San Francisco region, made appointments of alcaldes during his tenure in office. Commodore Sloat's short tour of duty in California, however, gave him little opportunity to Americanize the alcalde system or interfere appreciably with their decisions or administrations.[41]

When Commodore Robert F. Stockton succeeded Commodore Sloat as military governor of California on July 27, 1846, a more vigorous policy of governmental administration was adopted with the result that many alcaldes were replaced with American appointees.[42] The division of California into three sectors with a military com-

[41] A Law, John B. Montgomery, Aug. 16, 1846, Bancroft Library. Microcopy C-A, reel 1.

[42] General Order, R. F. Stockton, Los Angeles, Sept. 2, 1846, *U.S. Gov. Doc. Ser. 531*, p. 8.

WALTER COLTON
A Naval chaplain with Commodore Stockton, he was appointed the
first alcalde of Monterey, California. From an old engraving.

PETER H. BURNETT

Elected the first governor of California in 1849.
Courtesy of the Bancroft Library.

STEPHEN J. FIELD

Served as alcalde of Yubaville; later was appointed
the first United States Supreme Court Justice from
California. Courtesy of the Bancroft Library.

mander for each, by Commodore Stockton, had
the effect of bringing the military government into
closer contact with local administration. Although
no laws were issued to this effect, the alcaldes were
under the control of the military governor. In
cases where American alcaldes were appointed,
only the presence of American military forces
enabled them to retain their position. It was one of
the functions of the military government in California to lend support to local administrative
units when needed.[43] This point was strongly made
by Lieutenant W. T. Sherman, the assistant
adjutant general, in a letter to Colonel John D.
Stevenson at Los Angeles. He stated:

> Your several letters of the eleventh instant are received,
> and I am directed in replying to the several subjects to
> which they relate to inform you that your views are correct
> as to the assistance we should afford the civil. The civil
> officers would without doubt be most willing to shift upon
> military commanders the disagreeable labor of arresting
> and quartering their criminals, but this must not be per-
> mitted. Officers in command are not only expected to aid
> civil officers who are unable to enforce their decrees or
> execute the laws without such aid, and even there a sound
> discretion should be exercised as to the nature and amount
> of assistance to be afforded. The degree of assistance to be
> given by the military government to the civil government
> necessarily is dependent upon the attitude of the people
> towards the civil government and the attitude of the mili-
> tary commandant in the area.[44]

[43] Montgomery, San Francisco, to Pedro Chevoga, San Jose, Aug.
12, 1846, B. L. Microcopy C-A, reel 1.

[44] Sherman, Monterey, to Stevenson, Los Angeles, Aug. 23, 1846.
"Stevenson Collection."

Once appointments of local alcaldes were made in key places and control of the province of California considered more secure, Commodore Stockton arranged an election to be held on September 15, 1846, for alcaldes.[45] One of the early and wiser appointments made by Commodore Stockton was the appointment of Walter Colton as alcalde of Monterey. On September 15, 1846, Colton received a plurality of sixty-eight votes to become the duly elected alcalde of Monterey.[46] As first alcalde of the district he assumed the Judgeship of First Instance and therefore received appeals from other alcaldes throughout the district.[47]

The fees charged by the alcaldes under the Spanish and Mexican system for various licenses, legalizing signatures and opening wills was continued by Americans.[48] This had the effect of furnishing the alcalde with a little "side money," but was viewed by some as a form of graft. One contemporary visitor to Monterey made this point:

> A salutary system of police had been established in the town [Monterey] the reverend alcalde was a terror to evil doers [sic]. Woe betide the pockets of those who slaughtered cattle at their doorsteps, or the rollicking gentry vaulting at full speed through the streets, or drunken Indians, or quiet persons in back rooms amusing

---

[45] Proclamation, Stockton, Los Angeles, Aug. 12, 1846, "Gillespie Collection."

[46] Colton, *Three Years in California*, p. 17.

[47] *The Californian*, Monterey, Aug. 27, 1846.

[48] Judge H. S. Brown, "Statement of Early Days in California," MSS in Bancroft Library.

themselves at monte – for down came the ivory headed
[*sic*] cane – "alcalde de Monterey" – like a talisman; and
with a pleasant smile he would sweep the white and yellow
dross into his captious [*sic*] pockets. Others were maulked
[*sic*] in damages or made to quarry stone for the school-
house; but, whether native or foreign, the rod fell im-
partially on their pockets, and all, more or less, contributed towards the new California college. These
measures were not relished at first by the natives, but in
the end they discerned the wisdom of a prompt and just
administration of the laws, and became devoted admirers
to the indefatigable alcalde.[49]

The problem of quartering prisoners because of
the lack of proper jail facilities plagued the alcaldes in California both under the Spanish and
Mexican rule, as well as during the period of
military government. It was found expedient by
alcaldes to impose heavy fines upon individuals
being sentenced rather than send them to jail.[50]
Alcalde Colton, however, formed a labor gang and
put the prisoners to work erecting the first "important" building in California, Colton Hall.
Here in 1849 the Constitutional Convention met
and framed a state constitution.[51]

The Californian, the first newspaper printed in
English in California, of which Walter Colton
was the co-editor, listed several areas where the
alcalde and the council of Monterey legislated for
the district. Laws were passed regulating the sell-

---

49 Lt. Henry Augustus Wise, *Los Gringos,* p. 131.
50 T. Butler King, Washington, to John M. Clayton, Washington,
Mar. 22, 1850, *U.S. Gov. Doc. Ser. 577,* p. 2.
51 Colton, *Three Years in California,* p. 94.

ing of liquor and prohibiting gambling. A news item in the *Californian* of August 29, 1846, called attention first to the superior tribunal of Monterey which took cognizance of all cases that came within the alcalde's decision in that district. Then, by way of some judicial promotion, this statement was made:

> The magistrates of Monterey sit daily and give patient attention to all cases that are brought before them. On them devolves the civil police of the town and district. Their investigations are thorough, their decisions prompt, and impartial. Their office is open from nine o'clock a.m. to four o'clock p.m.[52]

Alcalde Colton became a credit to his office and was highly respected by both Californians and Americans. It appears from his many decisions that the welfare of the community was his main objective, and he scrupulously interpreted the law toward that end. When a man of questionable reputation appeared before him asking for a warrant for the arrest of his mistress who had run away and carried off some valuable jewelry, Alcalde Colton refused to grant his request. He stated:

> And as to the warrant, I should issue none, and would not if she had carried off everything in his house and him, too; for I should consider the community quit of two persons who could in no way benefit its morals.[53]

Colton was also careful not to violate social cus-

---

[52] *The Californian,* Monterey, Aug. 27, 1846.
[53] Colton, *Three Years in California,* p. 61.

toms and traditions of the Californians. Aware of
the strong family ties among Californians and the
almost blind obedience of children to the parents,
Alcalde Colton severely chastised an unmarried
son for striking his mother. Colton stated:

> A California mother complained to me today that her
> son, a full-grown youth, had struck her. Usage here allows
> a mother to chastise her son as long as he remains unmar-
> ried and lives at home, whatever may be his age, and
> regards a blow inflicted on a parent as a high offense. I
> sent for the culprit; laid his crime before him, for which
> he seemed to care but little; and ordered him to take off
> his jacket, which was done. And putting a reata into the
> hands of his mother, whom nature had endowed with
> strong arms, directed her to flog him. Every cut of the
> reata made the fellow jump from the floor. Twelve lashes
> were enough; the mother did her duty, as I had done mine,
> the parties were dismissed. No further complaint from that
> quarter.[54]

The introduction of the jury system into the
alcalde court can be credited to Alcalde Colton of
Monterey. Certainly the use of "hombres buenos"
under the Mexican system was in itself a quasi-
jury.[55] The breach between the two was not so wide
as to make introduction of the jury system difficult.
Therefore, in September of 1846, Colton empaneled the first jury with some measure of success. Colton's account states:

> One-third of the jury were Mexicans, one-third were
> Californians and the other third Americans. This mixture

---

[54] *Ibid.,* p. 192.
[55] Halleck, *Digest of Mexican Laws,* pp. 21-3.

may have the better answered the ends of justice, but I was apprehensive at one time it would embarrass the proceedings; for the plaintiff spoke in English, the defendant in French, the jury, save for the Americans, Spanish, and the witnesses all languages known to California. But through the silent attention which prevailed, the tact of Mr. Hartnell, who acted as interpreter, and the absence of young lawyers, we got along very well.[56]

The ingenuity of the alcalde was taxed from time to time for various reasons, foremost being to obtain honest testimony. Swearing on the Bible had some affect among witnesses, but at times stronger "medicine" had to be used. One alcalde in Colton's district was faced with a witness who did not have the best reputation for veracity. According to Colton:

> He thought it best to swear him pretty strongly; so he swore him on the Bible, on the Cross, by the Holy Angels, by the Blessed Virgin, and on the *twelve* Evangelists. I have written him for some information about eight of his evangelists, as I have no recollection of having met with but four in my Biblical readings.[57]

The alcalde appointed at San Francisco was also a military officer, Lieutenant Washington A. Bartlett. During his rather stormy administration in which a citizens' committee accused him of misappropriation of funds, Alcalde Bartlett officially changed the name of the town from Yerba Buena to San Francisco.[58] Also within a month after

---

[56] Colton, *Three Years in California,* p. 47.
[57] *Ibid.,* p. 227.
[58] *The California Star,* San Francisco, Jan. 13, 1847.

Colton empaneled the first jury, Bartlett at San Francisco did likewise. Edwin Bryant, who succeeded Bartlett as alcalde, reported the trial as follows:

> The proceedings were a mixture, made up of common law, equity, and a sprinkling of military despotism – which last ingredient the court was compelled to employ, when entangled in the intricate meshes woven by the counsel for the litigants, in order to extricate himself.[59]

By the time General Stephen Watts Kearny assumed control of the military government in February, 1847, the empaneling of juries in alcalde courts was almost a well-established custom.

The naval officers appointed alcaldes by Commodore Stockton were removed when General Kearny became military governor of California.[60] In his proclamation to the people of California, Kearny indicated his plan to continue the existing laws (meaning Mexican laws) in force. He stated:

> The laws now in existence, and not in conflict with the Constitution of the United States, will be continued until changed by competent authority; and those persons who hold office will continue in the same for the present, provided they swear to support that Constitution, and to faithfully perform their duty.[61]

For the most part, civilians were appointed as alcaldes in replacement of the naval officers appointed by Stockton. In coastal sections of Califor-

---

[59] Edwin Bryant, *What I Saw in California,* p. 307.

[60] W. T. Sherman, *Memoirs,* p. 54.

[61] Proclamation, Kearny, Mar. 1, 1847, N. A. Microfilm 82, roll no. 1.

nia, whether alcaldes were appointed or elected, the military governor exercised a good deal of control over their official acts.[62] The interior sections, because of their remoteness, were relatively free from military interference. Particularly close watch, however, was kept by Governor Kearny over the acts of the alcaldes in the more heavily populated coastal sections. To the alcalde of San Diego, H. D. Fitch, Kearny promised military assistance in carrying out any of his judicial acts and virtually ordered that certain persons be fined and imprisoned.[63] John H. Nash, the alcalde of Sonoma, was ordered to reverse a decision and reinstate the defendant, Colonel Victor Burton, to his property and withdraw any damages ordered by the court.[64] Similarly the alcalde of San Jose, John Burton, was ordered to dismiss a case which had been earlier tried by the Mexican courts. Kearny further ordered that any suit decided by the former courts of the country was not to be retried by the alcaldes under the military government in California.[65]

General Kearny's successor, Colonel Richard Mason, assumed even closer supervision of all levels of government in California. He readily

[62] Mason, Monterey, to Stevenson, Los Angeles, June 1, 1847, "Stevenson Collection."

[63] Kearny, Monterey, to H. D. Fitch, San Diego, April 27, 1847. *U.S. Gov. Doc. Ser. 573,* p. 302.

[64] Kearny, Monterey, to John H. Nash, Sonoma, March 3, 1847, N. A. Microfilm 82, reel no. 1.

[65] Kearny, Monterey, to John Burton, San Jose, Mar. 26, 1847, *U.S. Gov. Doc. Ser. 573,* p. 392.

admitted his wide authority as military governor. Similarly, he did not feel a bit strange in exercising authority over the alcaldes and properly defined their function under military rule. He stated:

> In the present condition of affairs in California, the alcaldes are not "authorities of California", nor are they Mexican authorities. They are civil magistrates of California, and are therefore the "authorities of California" within their respective jurisdictions, subject to removal from office by the authority of the Governor, and from the circumstances which the country is at present placed, and that must necessarily be so.[66]

Mason conscientiously attempted to place trustworthy and capable people in the office of alcalde. By 1848 most of the alcaldeships in California were in the hands of Americans. A mere handful of alcaldes were native Californians.[67]

The Treaty of Guadalupe Hidalgo did not change the authority or status of the alcalde in California. With the adoption of the Mexican laws of 1837, the alcalde's position was made more secure, although in some areas attempts were made to abolish alcaldes altogether. This was almost carried into effect in San Francisco in the early part of 1849.[68]

---

[66] Mason, Monterey, to L. W. Boggs, Sonoma, June 2, 1847, N. A. Microfilm 82, roll no. 1.

[67] Juan and Andrés Angel were alcaldes at Santa Inez; J. Mariano Bonilla at San Luis Obispo; and Pedro C. Carrillo at Santa Barbara.

[68] Proclamation, Riley, Monterey, June 3, 1849, *U.S. Gov. Doc. Ser. 573*, pp. 776-780.

The effect of the gold rush on the alcaldes, was more noticeable. In the first place, the increased population in California created a need for more local government in the mushrooming mining camps. More alcaldes, therefore, served as magistrates, and, in the mining districts, they were almost universally elected to office.[69] Secondly, the alcaldes elected were usually Americans and almost completely uninformed of Mexican laws. They were, for the most part, free from interference from the military government. Thirdly, in the mining districts, the alcalde was relieved of his executive functions, a constable or sheriff being appointed to carry out his decrees and decisions.[70] A contemporary observer stated:

> Districts are set off, their boundary determined by local convention. An alcalde, or governor, is elected by popular suffrage, and an executive officer to carry into effect his decisions. There is no council or legislature. The alcaldes court is strictly a court of equity. He decides all matters of offense or individual rights. . . Murder is punishable by hanging; as is larceny, second or third offense. Smaller grades of crimes and misdemeanors, are punished by whipping, cropping, and banishment. The alcalde decides all matters of disputed claims. The system generally works well. Where all are so mutually interested in supporting the laws and good order, the decisions of the alcaldes are acquiesced with and enforced with little difficulty.[71]

The increased wealth of the area, which caused

---

[69] M'Collum, *California As I Saw It*, p. 51.
[70] Riley, Root, *Journal of Travels*, p. 129-31.
[71] M'Collum, *op. cit.*

a sudden inflation, was attended by a wave of
lawlessness. Fines were not considered too serious,
and the case of one, John C. Pulas, who was fined
five dollars by Alcalde Leavenworth in San Francisco for swearing in court was typical. Not having
anything smaller than a doubloon (worth sixteen
dollars), Pulas handed it to the court with instructions for it to keep the change and he would take
it out in more swearing at a later time.[72]

As the mining camps increased in number, and
the population of the province soared, some attention was given to the establishment of civil government independent of the military government.
Miners' courts soon gave way to the alcalde, who
was elected as the judicial authority in many mining districts. Once elected, the alcalde's word was
the final judicial ruling on a case, since there was
no appeal. This sometimes seemed unjust to some
people, but it was much more preferable to the
swift miners' court and the evil consequences of
"lynch law." A visitor to the mining regions
stated:

> Whenever a sufficient assemblage of miners exists to be
> thought worthy of judicial attention, an alcalde or justice
> of the peace was appointed, who presides over the judiciary
> department with almost as unlimited sway as an emperor.
> And although in addition to an alcalde a sheriff is ap-
> pointed to be a permanent officer and cases are almost
> universally tried by jury, which is summoned by the sheriff,
> yet they are generally selected of a stamp congruous to the
> feeling of the alcalde. From the decisions, no appeal can

[72] Guy J. Giffen, *California Expeditions*, p. 84.

ever be made, whether right or wrong. I would likewise remark, that decisions are apt to be made against a party having the most gold, and especially if one of the partners is rather low in circumstance.[73]

The ingredients needed for alcalde success in the mining districts were simply a feeling for the underdog and summary handling of the particularly heinous crimes of horse stealing and claim jumping. Visitors in the mining districts were impressed by the presence of law and order. There were dstricts with two thousand or more people and sufficient wealth to tempt many into stealing. The severity with which claim jumping and stealing were dealt with made many of the mining districts relatively free of that sort of crime. It was reported by one visitor that:

> A man may dig a hole in the dry ravines, and, as long as he leaves a shovel, pick or crowbar, to show that he still intends working it, he is safe from trespass. His tools may remain there for months without being disturbed. There are, of course, exceptions to the rules, but they are not frequent. . .[74]

This situation prevailed more during the early days of the gold rush in 1848, and the early part of 1849. The exceptions began to appear with the great migration of 1849.[75]

A distinctive feature of the alcalde courts during

---

[73] Root, *op. cit.*

[74] California: *Its Past History: Its Present Position; Its Future Prospects*, p. 161.

[75] Leonard Kip, *California Sketches With Recollections of the Gold Mines*, p. 40.

the gold rush period was their swift justice. The
American alcaldes, not being hampered by any
particular laws, would insist that cases be summed
up quickly by the lawyers.[76] Decisions by both jury
and alcalde were definitely not long in coming.
One alcalde, who was Judge of the First Instance,
and who gained a reputation for swift, unusual,
but fair justice, was William B. Almond of San
Francisco. His court was in session from eight
o'clock in the morning until ten or eleven at night,
the result being that he had difficulty in keeping
clerks. One clerk, stating that he was killing himself at the pace demanded of him by the court,
resigned after a month's work. Judge Almond,
however, pushed through the cases at an extremely
rapid pace. He allowed each lawyer five minutes
to plead his case and no more. If the lawyer insisted on more time, Judge Almond stated that he
would allow him the time, but that the court would
inevitably decide the case against his client. Needless to say, the attorney summed up his case in the
five minutes allowed.[77]

Professional people in California during the
gold rush were few and therefore their services
were priced quite high. Generally, the price of one
ounce of gold (sixteen dollars) was charged for
the most basic service by the lawyers, doctors, or
dentists. The services of a lawyer, involving an
hour or two before an alcalde, amounted to a

---

[76] Field, *Personal Reminiscences,* pp. 28-31.

[77] Peter H. Burnett, *Recollection and Opinions of An Old Pioneer,*
pp. 333-334; Belden, "Statement of Historical Facts," p. 4.

hundred dollars or more. Court costs, which were paid by the losing party, amounted to an ounce to the alcalde, an ounce to the sheriff and a half ounce to each juror. Despite the extravagance of justice in California, many cases were brought before alcaldes and Judges of First Instance.[78]

Among the many Americans appointed to the office of alcalde was Stephen J. Field, who was later to become chief justice of California and the first U.S. Supreme Court justice from California.[79] As alcalde of Yubaville (now Marysville), Field simply followed American patterns of justice. He stated:

> I knew nothing of Mexican law; did not pretend to know anything of it; but I knew that the people had elected me to act as a magistrate and looked to me for the preservation of order and settlement of disputes; I did my best that they should not be disappointed. . . In civil cases, I always called a jury, if the party desired one; in criminal cases, when the offense was of a high grade, I went through the form of calling a grand jury, and having an indictment found; and in all cases I appointed an attorney to represent the people, and also the accused. . .[80]

Field also confessed that the premium placed on quick justice at the time in California forced him to make immediate decisions in cases where there was some inconclusive evidence. The fact that the alcalde's decisions were accepted prevented further conflict and contributed to the public welfare.[81]

---

[78] M'Collum, *California As I Saw It*, p. 43.
[79] Field, *Personal Reminiscences*, p. 27.
[80] *Ibid.*
[81] *Ibid.*

Among the American alcaldes there were several who were particularly noted at times for their
sagacity and at other times for their peculiarities.
Neither the court procedure nor the sentences
meted out by the alcalde courts corresponded to
anything found in either American or Mexican
courts at the time. A well known and respected
alcalde was William Blackburn, former Virginia
cabinetmaker, who was appointed alcalde of the
district of Santa Cruz. Blackburn became noted
for the originality of his decisions, which were
technically irregular, but were firmly based on
common sense and, therefore, greatly appealing to
the people.[82] A case was brought before Blackburn
involving a vaquero who had accidentally knocked
down a pregnant woman while he was engaged in
saving her life by intercepting a wild steer that
was rushing at her. The fall and excitement caused
her to lose her child. The husband of the woman
thereupon brought suit against the vaquero for
damages and during the trial there was a great
emphasis placed on the loss of the child. After
hearing both sides, Alcalde Blackburn solemnly
announced his decision, and ordered that the
vaquero should put the woman back in the same
condition as he found her and that the costs of the
trial be paid by the husband.[83]

Frank Bates, the alcalde at Sutter's Fort, or

---

[82] Elisha Oscar Crosby, *Reminiscences of California and Guatemala,
From 1849 to 1864,* p. 113.
[83] *Ibid.*

Sacramento, was notorious for his odd procedure and fines. A contemporary of Bates stated:

> Frank's penalty for any petty crime was usually a fine of six to twelve bottles of Byas's ale, according to the gravity of the offense and the necessities of the crowd in attendance. They were worth at the time half an ounce a piece, and six bottles of ale was equivalent to $48 or $50. The penalty was paid on the spot and the ale was brought in and drunk by the court and its friends. I have known him to impose this penalty a number of times.[84]

In another case, before Alcalde Almond, who was Judge of the First Instance, a judgment of two hundred dollars was entered for the plaintiff. The counsels for the plaintiff thereupon announced to Almond that they had charged two hundred dollars for fees and their client was therefore making nothing from the judgment. The judge then called his clerk and told him to enter the judgment for three hundred dollars. The defense attorneys immediately arose and attempted to argue the matter, but Judge Almond warned them that if they did he would raise the judgment to five hundred dollars.[85] These were peculiar decisions, but seemingly they were in keeping with the unnatural situation caused by the gold rush in California.

Alcalde rule in California answered the need for local justice and government both in sparsely populated California under the Spanish and Mexican governments, and in the frenzy of the gold

---

[84] *Ibid.*
[85] Brown, "Statement of Early Days in California."

rush during the American military government. When the state constitution was adopted and city government established in California, the alcalde had to yield his ancient authority and varied powers. The last alcalde of San Francisco, Alfred Geary, was elected mayor under the city's first charter on January 1, 1850.[86] Similarly, in other cities in California, former alcaldes were elected mayors of cities – Stephen Clark Foster, alcalde of Los Angeles, was elected mayor in 1854.[87] An institutional link, therefore, existed between the offices of alcalde and mayor in California, and yet this link has resulted in virtually no carry-over features of the alcalde in the office of mayor. Once the state government was formed, the alcalde with his multifarious duties was gone, and the Anglo-American principle of separation of powers was adopted throughout the state.

[86] Riley, Monterey, to J. W. Geary, San Francisco, August 1, 1849, *U.S. Gov. Doc. Ser. 573,* p. 797; Soule, *Annals of San Francisco,* p. 724.

[87] Stephen Clark Foster, "Alcalde of Los Angeles," MS in Bancroft Library, pp. 16-19.

Civil vs. Military—
Military Government Ends

Normal distaste for military government, especially one administered by an enemy, was a factor the American forces hoped to counteract with a benign attitude towards Californians and their customs. In the brief administration of Commodore John D. Sloat no opposition towards the Americans was encountered nor did the people seem greatly alarmed or dissatisfied with the American occupation.[1]

The only serious manifestations of discontent on the part of the Californians appeared in the uprising in Los Angeles during Commodore Robert F. Stockton's tenure as military governor, which almost resulted in a full-scale war. This contempt for American military government was partially fomented by the commander of the southern district in California, Lieutenant Archibald Gillespie, whose orders struck at the heart of California customs and traditions.[2] This uprising, however, was the last organized opposition to military control by the Californians. The record shows no

[1] Sloat, Monterey, to George Bancroft, Washington, July 31, 1846, *U.S. Gov. Doc. Ser. 493*, pp. 640-42.

[2] Juan Flores' Proclamation, Oct. 1, 1846, National Archives Microfilm 89, roll no. 33.

evidence of further dissatisfaction by the Californians to United States rule, although from time to time alarmists would write to the military governors of California regarding suspected revolts among the natives.

After their near-successful revolt against the Stockton regime of military government, the Californians reconciled themselves to military government and eventual incorporation into the United States. That they were not noticeably dissatisfied with military government in California is not difficult to understand. In the first place, the military governors did very little to disturb the function and administration of government as it operated under Mexico. The alcaldes remained the local administrative officers and the military governors exercised no more authority than their Mexican predecessors had. Secondly, Californians with vested interests were placated and appointed to responsible governmental positions. Enough native Californians were retained in secondary governmental posts not to alarm the people greatly. Thirdly, increased American migration to California soon placed native Californians in the position of a subdued minority, especially once the gold rush got under way. Their dissatisfaction, if indeed voiced, was soon submerged by the American desire for civil government.[3]

The more serious manifestations of dissatisfaction with the military government in California

---

[3] *The Californian*, Monterey, Aug. 15, 1846; Mar. 13, 1847.

came from the American residents of the province. Prior to American occupation, a group of highly dissatisfied American immigrants in the Sonoma area resorted to open rebellion against the Mexican government. Somewhat placated with American occupation under Commodore Sloat and the promise of "civil government" under Commodore Stockton, the Americans in California expected something more than military government supporting former Mexican laws. The Stockton proclamation which ordered an election for local officers and promised a civil government, and likewise, the Fremont proclamation declaring civil government in force, were hailed by the American residents as pillars of civil freedom.[4] When General Kearny assumed the military governorship in California, however, it soon became apparent to all that "civil government" was a term loosely used by military governors in California. Yet the seed of discontent appeared even before Kearny took command. In the *California Star* of January 23, 1847, the editorial declared that the alcaldes in California were assuming unauthorized power:

> If any alcalde has the right, however, to make a single law or rule, or to make the slightest change in one, he certainly has the legislative power of the country in his hands, and has the right to adopt a whole code at once. This is not the case, they do not have such power, and they must know that they have not.[5]

---

[4] *Ibid.,* Oct. 17, 1846; *The California Star,* San Francisco, Feb. 9, 1847.

[5] *The California Star,* San Francisco, Jan. 23, 1847.

A month later the same paper again attacked the alcaldes.

> The cry is for an effective judiciary in California
> . . . the present system is worse than none – it is worse
> than anarchy. We have alcaldes all over the country, as-
> suming the powers of the legislatures, issuing and pro-
> mulgating their bandos, laws and orders, and oppressing
> the people. Many of these dignitaries have never before
> been accustomed to civil duties, and a little office, and their
> belief that there is a prospect of a greater, has completely
> befuddled them. The most nefarious scheme, treachery and
> speculating have been practiced by some that was never
> disclosed to the light of heaven.[6]

The article then made the suggestion that the province be divided up into counties with each having its elected justice of the peace. Three judicial districts, each with a district judge should be created for a proper judiciary system in California, the editorial claimed.[7]

Shortly after issuing his proclamation to the people of California, General Kearny was faced with the problem of extinguishing the flame of representative civil government begun by the proclamation of Stockton. On March 6, 1847, the people of San Francisco met in a public meeting and announced a plan for a legislative council wherein each district in California was represented by at least one member.[8] They then proceeded to elect J. A. T. Dunleavy as their representative.

---

[6] *Ibid.*, Feb. 13, 1847.

[7] *Ibid.*

[8] *Ibid.*, Mar. 6, 1847; Kearny, Monterey, to Edwin Bryant, San Francisco, Mar. 4, 1847, *U.S. Gov. Doc. Ser. 573*, pp. 289-91.

This also occurred in Sonoma. When a copy of the proceedings reached General Kearny he immediately dispatched letters to the alcaldes of the cities of Sonoma and San Francisco stating:

> I will thank you in reply to say to these gentlemen, and all others interested and concerned in the matter, that I have not called for any such council, nor do I at present contemplate doing so.[9]

Thus Kearny quietly and effectively squashed this earliest attempt at a representative legislative council. The northern areas, however, and primarily San Francisco, continued in their dissatisfaction with the military government and furnished the initiative in demanding civil representative government.

Many of the complaints lodged against the military government in California resulted from tariff policy. The early moderate customs charges established were scaled upward by Washington instructions of 1847. Fortunately, the military governor only partially complied with this tariff. But even the reduced customs charges drew complaints. The usually loyal Alcalde Colton stated:

> Through the exactions of the custom house the comforts and necessities of life were oppressively taxed. No article of food or rainment could escape this forced contribution; it reached the plow of the farmer, the anvil of the smith; the blanket that protected your person, the salt that seasoned your food, the shingle that roofed your cabin and the nail that bound your coffin.[10]

[9] Kearny to Bryant, Mar. 6, 1847, *ibid.*, p. 290.
[10] Colton, *Three Years in California*, p. 394.

It will be readily agreed that tariff duties generally affect all levels of society, but Reverend Colton's account perhaps shows oppression that did not exist. Tariff rates in California during the American occupation were significantly lower than those of the former Mexican schedules and appreciably below United States tariffs. Something bordering on "free trade" was desired by the Americans in California.[11]

Probably the most annoying aspect of the customs charges was their lack of uniformity. One contemporary who experienced this stated:

> At San Francisco I had to pay a duty of 75¢ per gallon on brandy and two days after being in the port of Monterey, the duties on brandy of the same quality were 50¢ per gallon. I protested in paying and I now protest for the surplus of duties which I was made to pay in the port of San Francisco.[12]

The fact that the military governors greatly modified the tariff instructions coming from Washington doubtless added to the confusion and non-uniformity of tariff rates. One section of the tariff of 1847 which remained unchanged in California was the twenty per cent ad valorum duty on all goods arriving from foreign countries.[13] This duty, which was part of the United States tariff structure at the time, seemed oppressive to the Americans in California, who began recalling their early

---

[11] Proclamation, Kearny, Mar. 1, 1847, N. A. Microfilm 82, roll no. 1.

[12] Statement, Jules Chanon, "California Military Government Collection," Bancroft Library.

[13] Circular, Mason, Oct. 14, 1847, N. A. Microfilm 82, roll no. 1.

school histories concerning "taxation without representation." An article in *The California Star* stated:

> We are paying at present a duty of 20% ad valorum, for all goods arriving at our ports from all parts of the globe. We deem it an act of justice for the government of the United States to exonerate us from this law, which was evidently intended to bear on the enemies and not on the friends of that government. It certainly falls heavy on poor immigrants just stepping in a new country.[14]

Certainly the concern here could not have been entirely for the "poor immigrant," for quite obviously the residents in California would be subject to a twenty per cent increase in the purchase of goods of foreign lands.

If hope for a civil government seemed remote under General Kearny, it was virtually nonexistent under his successor, Colonel Mason. To Mason, California was undeniably under military government. Congress had the only right to establish civil government, after the territory had been properly annexed to the United States.[15] Opposition to the military rule administered by Colonel Mason began to appear in print in June, 1847. An article in *The Californian* of June 5, which claimed to express the sentiments of American residents in California, attacked "military despotism" and expressed a hope that the territorial government

---

[14] *The California Star,* San Francisco, Apr. 1, 1848.

[15] Mason, Monterey, to L. W. Boggs, Sonoma, June 2, 1847, *U.S. Gov. Doc. Ser. 573,* pp. 317-18.

promised by Kearny would be affected. The article stated:

> We hear much of military despotism. There is no form of government that has more horrors, or sounds more harsh to an American. . . The American residents in California are fully aware that they are of necessity under military law, nor do they expect to enjoy all of the blessings and facilities which a well regulated civil government could afford them, but they do expect to have all of the advantages that could be afforded by a military government. We have no disposition to complain of what has been done. All the circumstances considered, we doubt whether things could have been done much better. But it is the duty of all to profit by experience, and what has been done amiss should be changed.[16]

The appointment of an alcalde to the district of San Francisco by Colonel Mason soon after his succession to command aroused the people of San Francisco, and they assembled at a meeting to protest. The governor's appointee, however, was retained in office. The circular printed to announce to the American residents the forthcoming protest meeting is interesting:

> THE PEOPLE'S RIGHT SIFTED BY INTRIGUE. PEOPLE OF SAN FRANCISCO RALLY YOUR RIGHTS! A majority of your number have petitioned the governor of the territory to appoint John Townsend, Esq., to succeed Mr. Bryan, Esq. as alcalde of this district. Intrigue has defeated the voice of the people. George Hyde is appointed! Will you submit to this? The unrevoked proclamation of General Stockton gives you the privilege of electing alcaldes for yourselves – the laws of California guarantee the same

---

[16] *The Californian,* San Francisco, June 5, 1847.

right. Assemble at Brown's hotel at seven o'clock this evening, and assert your rights.[17]

Another sore point was the long overdue payment for property, horses and supplies taken by the United States troops from private citizens in California. Colonel Mason urged payment, warning the Washington authorities that:

> The claimants, native and foreigners, [were] loud and clamorous and [excited] a great deal of dissatisfaction and bad feeling in the country towards [the] government.[18]

Several years, however, were to elapse before a proper examination of the debts resulted in payment.[19]

Greater "dissatisfaction and bad feeling" resulted however, from Mason's arbitrary measures in deposing a duly elected alcalde of Los Angeles on the recommendation of Colonel Stevenson, the military commandant. An American, Stephen C. Foster, was then appointed and Mason was thus assured of having "the entire review of the alcaldes' acts." [20]

Although never considered seriously as a threat, sentiment for independent government for California was nevertheless present, and to a great extent

---

[17] James A. Hardie, San Francisco, to Mason, Monterey, May 30, 1847, "Archives of California," p. 109.

[18] Mason, Monterey, to R. Jones, Washington, June 18, 1847, *U.S. Gov. Doc. Ser. 503*, p. 519.

[19] C. F. Smith, Charles Thomas, and R. B. Lee, Washington, to The Senate, and House of Representatives, Apr. 18, 1855, *U.S. Gov. Doc. Ser. 821*, pp. 3-5.

[20] Stevenson, Los Angeles, to Mason, Monterey, Dec. 19, 1847, "Archives of California," p. 128.

an outgrowth of dissatisfaction with military government. One of the earliest reports of any organized attempt to establish independent government in California came to Governor Mason in a dispatch from Charles White, the alcalde of San Jose. This dispatch, dated March 4, 1848, informed Mason of a party of sixty men who were daily recruiting new members to their cause, which seemingly was to attack the prison at Monterey and release the prisoners. This, of course, would greatly augment their number, and aid them in their plan to establish an independent government in California.[21] White also stated:

> They are well armed and the good people in the country stand in fear of exposing these people as they might kill them.[22]

This group may have been precursors to the "Hounds" who terrorized San Francisco a year later, but the subsequent dispatches reveal nothing more of their activities. Several months after White's dispatch, Mason received a letter from William Leidesdorff stating that the people opposing the appointment of George Hyde as alcalde of San Francisco were advocates of an independent government in California. He states that they were anxious to get in possession of the office in order to execute their plans which were supported by a "strong Mormon influence."[23] But again no overt

---

[21] "Archives of California," p. 149.

[22] *Ibid.*, p. 169.

[23] William A. Leidesdorff, San Francisco, to Mason, Monterey, 1848, *ibid.*, p. 68.

steps were taken. Some people were convinced that the threat of an independent California was largely imaginary.

H. W. Halleck, the Secretary of State under both Colonel Mason and General Riley, states that independent government was all nonsense, and it was doomed to fail because the people would not submit to be taxed for its support.[24] The first governor of the State of California, Peter Burnett, further stated that:

> There was not the slightest ground for the charge that the people of California desired to establish an independent government.[25]

This was merely a fiction, he declared, created by suspicion in the minds of informants of the military government.

Discontent with military rule became more outspoken beginning in 1848. More and stronger appeals and editorials for the establishment of civil government began to appear in the columns of *The Californian*.[26] The inadequacy of the alcalde system was the subject of one heated editorial:

> If a man has a complaint against another, he must act as constable and bring him before the alcalde (if he is willing to come), who in conformity with previous instructions "administers the laws according to the former usages of the country" which "usages" he and the scape-grace under trial

---

[24] Halleck, Monterey, to Stevenson, Los Angeles, June 1, 1849, "Leidesdorff Papers."

[25] Burnett, "Correspondence and Papers," II.

[26] Dec. 29, 1847; Jan. 5, Feb. 2, 1848.

know as much about as we do of benighted Japan, and the
will of the alcalde alone becomes law, and consequently we
have as many laws and sub-laws in California as we have
alcaldes and sub-alcaldes! [27]

Another editorial which placed the conquest of
California on a more personal basis, shrewdly
quoted from Kearny's proclamation concerning the
establishment of civil government.

What, we hear our people everywhere inquiring, what
have we acquired by our conquest here in this country?
. . . In view of our civil rights, in view of the security
of person and property, and in view of our sacred rights
and privileges secured to us by the fundamental laws of
our government, we must say we have acquired nothing,
but have lost everything. . . We know nothing of the
design of the present executive in reference to the organization of the civil government but we do know that the
people very much desire such an organization. And we
also know, that it is the "*wish* and *design* of the United
States to provide for them, a free government with the
least possible delay." [28]

Mason answered his critics several times in the
pages of the newspapers stating that a treaty of
peace with Mexico was *sine qua non* to the establishment of civil government in California. Furthermore, he stated, Congress had the sole authority
of establishing a territorial government.

During the summer months of 1848, the American residents in California eagerly awaited the
news of the treaty of peace with Mexico. In the

[27] *Ibid.*, Dec. 29, 1847.
[28] *Ibid.*, Jan. 5, 1848.

excitement of the gold rush, the sentiment for civil government was, however, somewhat squelched. News of gold discoveries replaced editorials demanding civil freedom.

News of the Treaty of Guadalupe Hidalgo was received by Colonel Mason on August 1 and appeared in *The Californian* August 4 under the headline "Glorious News." To the proponents of civil government in California this was the moment they had been waiting for. They claimed ecstatically:

> The prospective view is grand, beyond all possible calculation. The imagination is lost in wonder, when we attempt to look forward and judge the future by the past.[29]

This hope, however, soon turned into bitter resentment, for the military government continued in control for more than a year, amid the most vitriolic statements against it. Although Colonel Mason (along with Commodore Jones) had promised a representative provisional government in default of Congressional action, he continued to administer the military government until he was relieved by General Riley in April of 1849.[30]

The clamor for civil government increased, and virtually every issue of the *California Star and Californian* included an article which urged the "Californians" to take action. On December 2 an article reported the inability of the military gov-

---

[29] *Ibid.,* Aug. 14, 1848.

[30] *The California Star and Californian,* San Francisco, Dec. 23, 1848.

ernment to cope with a murder occurring in the mining districts. The article stated:

> The late tragedy enacted in a mining district affords still another melancholy instance of outraged law. It proclaims, too, our inability as a people to restrain lawlessness by offering rewards for human heads, while, as now, without the usual power to affect the punishment of crime. It but strongly urges upon our countrymen the necessity of speedy measures for the organization of some kind of government — the framing of some law which may hold in terror evil doers, and most earnestly demands an ever attending execution of the severest penalties attached to criminal conduct, in a word, it brings vividly before us the momentous question — Shall we have a civil government in California? [31]

A fortnight later, on December 16, when word was received of Congress' inaction, mass meetings began to be staged in some of the northern districts of California in an effort to establish provisional government. In San Francisco the *California Star and Californian* urged the people to "take steps."

> The arrival of the "St. Mary's" has doubtlessly settled the question relative to California territorial organization, and the people of this territory may set about preparing for themselves a provisional government, or suffer from the neglect of the matter which every day makes of more importance. A large enthusiastic meeting of the citizens of the pueblo of San Jose is the first preparatory movement of the kind that has yet taken place. San Francisco should give evidence of her approbation of the measure, and public demonstrations in every quarter will immediately follow. The cause is urgent and the times will admit of no delay.[32]

[31] *Ibid.*, Dec. 2, 1848.   [32] *Ibid.*, Dec. 16, 1848.

Similar mass meetings were held in Sacramento and Sonoma during the early months of 1849. Virtually the same full-voiced protests were made, in the same florid rhetoric, against the same loathed aspects of military government in California.

Nothing more clearly demonstrated the impotence of military rule in California than the wave of lawlessness and intimidation by mob rule that swept San Francisco during the first six months of 1849. Motivated somewhat by the pronouncements of General Persifor Smith,[33] stating that only the United States citizens be allowed in the gold fields, a group of ruffians and vagabonds, consisting largely of the discharged soldiers of Stevenson's battalion, organized a mutual benefit society in San Francisco, called the "Hounds" or the "Regulators." Composed mostly of murderers and thieves, the Hounds bound themselves in this organization to assist ostensibly one another in case of sickness or danger. The truth, however, was that they protected themselves against arrest, prosecution and penalties for their crimes. They assumed a sort of military organization, complete with discipline, largely a result of the military background of many of the members. Once their headquarters was established (at a tent called Tammany Hall) and officers elected, they began their outrages against the foreigners in the gold fields, mainly the people from Chile – or Chilenos. The

---

[33] P. Smith, Panama, to Marcy, Washington, Jan. 18, 1849.

Hounds had virtually the "run of the town" and would appear at restaurants and other business establishments in formidable groups taking what they wished without payment. They also extorted payments of money and jewels from people as a price to exempt them from their raids.[34]

The municipal authorities in San Francisco were almost powerless to stop the outrages of the Hounds. Some people suspected that the alcalde of San Francisco was in league with them. Colonel Mason and his seriously decreasing number of troops stood helplessly by and made no effort to stop the lawlessness in San Francisco. By July 15, however, the Hounds had caused sufficient damage to provoke responsible citizens of San Francisco to action. On that day the Hounds had topped their Sunday activities with a wanton riot in the Chileno quarters of San Francisco, seriously wounding many defenseless persons.[35] The next day the citizens of San Francisco had a meeting on Portsmouth Square and organized themselves into a police force for the apprehension of the Hounds. Twenty of the ringleaders were arrested and brought to trial before the alcalde, Dr. Leavenworth, but the local citizens, as a precautionary measure, had William M. Gwinn and James C. Ward lend assistance during the trial. Long and rather severe sentences were given the ringleaders

---

[34] *Alta California,* San Francisco, July 19, 1849; James Findla, "Statement of a Few Events," p. 8; Frank Soule, *The Annals of San Francisco,* p. 553-59.

[35] Findla, "Statement of a Few Events," p. 8.

of the Hounds, but the absence of adequate prisons and penitentiaries prevented the sentences from being carried out. Nonetheless, this action on the part of the citizens did effectively suppress the Hounds and restore a semblance of law and order. With the leaders sentenced and exiled, the rest of the Hounds judiciously drifted from San Francisco to other parts of the country.[36]

Adjournment of Congress in 1848 without providing a territorial government for California caused many people in California to wonder what the legal status of the province really was. Although many varied opinions were offered, two main theories seemed to draw the support of the people. The first was called the "administration theory" and was first proposed by Secretary of State James A. Buchanan in a dispatch of October 7, 1848. This theory supported the view that the military government should continue as the *de facto* government in California until such time as the Congress of the United States can provide proper territorial government. Buchanan stated:

> The termination of the war left an existing government, a government *de facto,* in full operation; and this will continue, with the presumed consent of the people, until Congress shall provide for them a territorial government. The great law of necessity justifies this conclusion. The consent of the people is irresistibly inferred from the fact that no civilized community can possibly desire to abrogate an existing government, when the alternative presented would be to place themselves in a state of anarchy, beyond

---

[36] Soule, *The Annals of San Francisco,* p. 557.

the protection of all laws, and reduce them to the unhappy necessity of submitting to the dominion of the strongest.[37]

This theory was accepted by Colonel Mason and the military commandant of the Pacific area, General Smith. Mason, in point of fact, had, in the dispatch of August 14, 1848, to the War Department, set forth similar views regarding his changed position in California. He stated that he was well aware that in continuing the military government in California he had no authority than that some form of government should continue until another was provided for by the administration in Washington.[38]

The other theory, which was referred to as "the settlers' theory" or Benton's Theory, drew the strongest support in California. Senator Thomas Hart Benton, from the state of Missouri, long considered to be the "spokesman of the west," entered into the argument concerning the legal status of California by propounding a theory which was seditious in tone, in a letter of August 27, 1848, entitled "To the People of California." This letter was published by the *New York Courier* and *Inquirer* of October 13, 1848, and was then printed by the *Alta California* on January 11, 1849. According to this theory, Benton stated that Mexican civil law in California had been suspended by the Treaty of Guadalupe Hidalgo. Furthermore, the

---

[37] James Buchanan, Washington, to William V. Vorhies, Washington, Oct. 7, 1848, *U.S. Gov. Doc. Ser. 573,* pp. 6-9.

[38] Mason, Monterey, to R. Jones, Washington, Aug. 19, 1848, N. A. Microfilm 82, roll no. 1.

province was now a part of the United States, and entitled to all of the laws of the country. Since Congress had failed to provide a government for the province, it was then the solemn duty of the people to provide some form of government for themselves. He stated:

The treaty with Mexico makes you citizens of the United States; Congress has not yet passed the laws to give you the blessings of our government; and it may be some time before it does so. In the meantime, while your condition is anomalous and critical, it calls for the exercise of the soundest discretion and the most exalted patriotism on your part. The temporary civil and military government established over you as a right of war is at an end. The edicts promulgated by your temporary governors Kearny and Mason (each an ignoramus) so far as these edicts went to change the law of the land, are null and void, and were so from the beginning, for the laws of the country remain in force unless altered by the proper legislative authority, and no legislative authority has as yet altered the laws which existed at the time of your conquest. The laws of California are still what they were, and are sufficient for your present protection, with some slight additions derived from your own voluntary consent and administered by officers of your own election. Having no lawful government, nor lawful officers, you may get none except by your own act; you can have none that can have authority over you except by your own consent. In fact, sanction must be the will of the majority. I recommend you to meet in convention – provide for a cheap and simple government – and take care of yourselves until Congress can provide for you.[39]

Benton then pointed to the success that the people

[39] *Alta California,* San Francisco, Jan. 11, 1849.

of Oregon had when they adopted his similar proposals some two years before. He said in effect
that: "they now have a territorial government and
you can also if you heed my advice." Appealing
almost immediately to the majority in California,
Benton's letter, however, was criticized for its bad
taste in condemning the military governors Kearny
and Mason.[40] Some protest was also raised by the
military elements in California.

On April 12, 1849, General Bennet Riley relieved
Colonel Mason as military governor of California.
He was well aware upon taking office of the ex-
plosive situation existing in California. Colonel
Mason had advised him to proceed with due cau-
tion. General Riley was, however, torn between
the two theories concerning the legal status of
California.[41] Mass meetings being held throughout
the northern areas of California demonstrated
majority support for the "Benton theory." Similarly, many of the protest editorials in the California
newspapers seemed to support this theory. Yet
Governor Riley was in a sense morally bound to
support the "administration's theory," being an
appointed officer of the executive branch of government.[42]

In San Francisco more trouble faced the governor. Two town councils and an elected body of
fifteen councilors, called the Legislative Assembly

---

[40] *Ibid.,* Jan. 18, 1849.

[41] Riley, Monterey, to R. Jones, Washington, June 30, 1849, *U.S.
Gov. Doc. Ser. 573,* p. 748.

[42] Marcy, Washington, to Riley, New York, Oct. 10, 1848, *U.S. Gov.
Doc. Ser. 557,* pp. 251-52.

of San Francisco, each claimed to be the legal government of the city. The alcalde, Dr. Leavenworth, refused to turn his office over to either of these bodies, and was supported by Generals Smith and Riley. Riley issued a proclamation declaring the Legislative Assembly of San Francisco illegal, and left the other two councils alone to settle their difficulties in their own way.[43] Another election, however, was needed before an alcalde and a town council of San Francisco could receive a majority support from the people of San Francisco.

Vacillating between the administration theory and the Benton theory, General Riley awaited congressional action before making his decision. Once again Congress adjourned without providing a government for California, and Governor Riley, on August 3, 1849, issued his proclamation whereby he reached a compromise between the two theories of California government.[44] The government, he claimed, was civil; he was a civil governor; the Mexican civil laws were therefore in force in California. The military, he said, recognized the existing civil government and its officers were pledged to support it. Riley then announced that since Congress had failed to organize a government for California, it was imperative then that a convention be called to frame a state constitution. In the meantime, the government of California, as it existed under Mexico, would be in effect, and he gave a brief summary of it.

[43] Proclamation, Riley, Monterey, June 4, 1849, *ibid.,* p. 749.

[44] Proclamation, Riley, Monterey, June 4, 1849, *U.S. Gov. Doc. Ser.* 573, pp. 776-80.

The convention, which was to consist of thirty-seven delegates was called to meet at Monterey on September 1 and the representation was apportioned as follows: the districts of San Luis Obispo, Santa Barbara and San Diego were to send two delegates each; Sacramento, Sonoma, San Joaquin and Los Angeles four each; and San Francisco, San Jose and Monterey, five each.[45] In reference to the supervision of the elections for delegates and extension of franchise the proclamation read:

> The local alcaldes and members of the *ayuntamientos* or town councils, will act as judges and inspectors of the elections. In case there should be less than three such judges and inspectors present in each of the places designated on the day of the election, the people will appoint some competent person to fill the vacancies. The polls will be open from ten a.m. to four p.m. or until sunset, if the judges deem it necessary.
>
> Every free male citizen of the United States and Upper California, twenty-one years of age, and actually resident in the district where the vote is offered, will be entitled to the right of suffrage. All citizens of Lower California who have been forced to come to this territory on account of rendering assistance to the American troops during the recent war with Mexico, should also be allowed to vote in the district where they actually reside.

Public reaction to Riley's proclamation was one of disapproval.[46] Enforcement of Mexican laws in California certainly did not appeal to the people, and, as for the calling of a convention to frame a state constitution and government, it was viewed

---

[45] *Ibid.*

[46] *Alta California,* San Francisco, June 14, 1849.

as stealing the limelight of representative government from the people. Some doubted his authority to call such a convention, as Riley himself, at times, must have. San Francisco, whose hostility was intensified over another proclamation the next day which was aimed at dissolving the legislative assembly, finally agreed to adopt the governor's terms respecting the convention only as a matter of expediency. The sentiment in other districts was somewhat the same. *The Placer Times* of June 26, stated:

> We are opposed to General Riley's assumption to exercise civil authority in this country, not so much because we think that his government would prove inimical to our rights and interests, but for the reason that his government is one that is legally incompatible with the Constitution of our country. We deny his right to govern us, but we cannot conceal from ourselves that the only remedy for the present deplorable situation is to pursue the course recommended in his proclamation so far as regards the organization of a State government.[47]

The accuracy with which General Riley anticipated the new administration of Zachary Taylor's views with respect to government in California leads one almost to suspect that he may have had some secret oral instructions. Riley, however, was an appointment made by the Polk administration. In March of 1849, Zachary Taylor's administration had taken office. The views expressed by the President, the Secretary of War and the president's special emissary to California, T. Butler King,

---

[47] *The Placer Times,* Sacramento, June 26, 1849.

were remarkably similar to the action taken by General Riley.[48] In a report to Congress, President Taylor stated:

> I did not hesitate to express to the people of those Territories my desire that each Territory should, if prepared to comply with the Constitution of the United States, form a plan of a State Constitution and submit the same to Congress, with prayer for admission into the Union as a state. . .[49]

Taylor, however, stated that this was just a suggestion and definitely could not be construed as an order or an official policy. On June 26, 1849, the new Secretary of War, George W. Crawford, expressed his sympathy for the people of California to form a government. He stated:

> The United States are doubly bound to admit the newly acquired Territories — California and New Mexico — into the confederacy of the states. It is not necessary to inquire whether the first step, in view of the proposed incorporation, should be taken by the people of the territories or by the invitation of Congress. In either case, the final judgment rests with Congress. Hence the opinion is advocated that it is the right of the people of California to assemble by their delegates and adopt a form of government which, if approved by Congress, may lead to their admission into the federal union as one of the confederated states.[50]

After receiving Riley's proclamation, Crawford

---

[48] Message from the President, Z. Taylor, Washington, Jan. 21, 1850; Geo. W. Crawford, Washington, to Riley, Monterey, June 26, 1849, *U.S. Gov. Doc. Ser. 557*, pp. 1-4, 276.

[49] Z. Taylor, Jan. 21, 1850, *ibid.*, pp. 1-4.

[50] Crawford, Washington, to Riley, Monterey, June 26, 1849, *ibid.*, p. 276.

answered him on August 24, stating that it was received "with great cheerfulness and alacrity."[51] T. Butler King, who arrived in California a few days following Riley's proclamation had orders to publicize the views of the President respecting the formation of any government "Republican in its character." He was also instructed to make it clear to the people that this government was to originate with themselves, "and without the interference of the Executive." Once framed, this government was then to be submitted to Congress for its approval.[52]

August 1 had been set by Riley as the election date for delegates to the convention. Although he had fixed the apportionment of representatives from each district, he did provide some latitude in cases where the sudden increase in population demanded more representation from a particular district. He stated:

> Should any district think itself entitled to a greater number of delegates than the above named, it may elect supernumeraries, who, on the organization of the convention, will be admitted or not, at the pleasure of that body.[53]

This provision was taken at its word by many of the districts. Extra delegates were elected and the problem of admitting them was the first faced at the convention. After various schemes of apportionment were presented to the group, the convention agreed to raise the membership from thirty-six

---

[51] Crawford, Washington, to Riley, Aug. 24, 1849, *ibid.*, pp. 262-63.
[52] John M. Clayton, Washington, to Thomas Butler King, Apr. 3, 1849, *U.S. Gov. Doc. Ser. 573*, pp. 9-11.
[53] Proclamation, Riley, June 4, 1849, *ibid.*, pp. 776-80.

to forty-eight. This necessarily altered the apportionment from each district, the increase going to the mining areas. The new apportionment was as follows: San Francisco and Sacramento districts were granted eight delegates; San Jose, seven; Monterey and San Joaquin six each; Los Angeles, five; San Diego and San Luis Obispo, two each; Sonoma, three; and Santa Barbara, one.[54]

Despite some bitter opposition to General Riley and his proclamation, many viewed the convention with optimism. The majority of the Americans in California desiring representative government was hopeful that the convention would answer its needs. One contemporary viewed the situation thus:

> On the first of August we go into an election for delegates for the Convention to form a State Constitution to meet at Monterey next month. We are also to vote for officers to enforce Mexican laws, the latter the Americans expect the Army officers do not believe in, all the Lawyers say the system will not work, and the only way is to form a State Legislature this autumn and make laws for ourselves, enforcing them independently of General Riley. This, General Riley has said he will not permit until it is sanctioned by Congress. How he is to help himself, I can't see. Mr. King of Georgia, who, by the way, is a very intelligent, good gentleman, has no doubt advised the cabinet on this subject. It is astonishing how ignorant the government and people generally are in regard to this country. You gentlemen who have been out here, ought to enlighten them. When you saw San Francisco last it had but five hundred inhabitants, it now has five thousand!!! [55]

---

[54] J. Ross Browne, *Report on the Debates in the Convention of California*, p. 22.

[55] Charles V. Gillespie, San Francisco, to A. H. Gillespie, Washington, July 30, 1849, "Gillespie Collection."

After the delegates had been elected from the various districts the problem concerning the transportation of them to the convention at Monterey loomed large. Many of the delegates, because of personal and business reasons as well as the expense and inconvenience involved in traveling to Monterey, seriously considered not attending.[56] Thomas Butler King, however, persuaded Commodore Jones to press into the service of the convention two United States ships, the United States steamer "Edith," to journey to San Diego and pick up delegates from the southern districts, and the brig "Fremont," to do the same in the northern areas. This plan, however, almost caused the failure of the convention, for the steamer "Edith" was wrecked on its passage, and a similar fate almost befell the brig, "Fremont." Somewhat delayed, the full delegation was present at the convention September 3.[57]

Among the delegates who had a prominent role in the convention were listed some of the most important people in California at the time. Present were such people as John A. Sutter, H. W. Halleck, William M. Gwinn, O. M. Wozencraft, Thomas O. Larkin, Stephen C. Foster, Abel Stearns, Hugo Reid, Lansford W. Hastings, Mariano Guadalupe Vallejo, Jose Antonio Carrillo, Robert Semple, Pacificus Ord, H. J. Dimmick and Elijah O. Crosby. The majority of the

[56] Foster, "Alcalde of Los Angeles," p. 16.

[57] Thomas ap C. Jones, San Francisco, to William B. Preston, Washington, Sept. 12, 1849; James McCormick, Monterey, to Thomas ap C. Jones, Aug. 26, 1849. *U.S. Gov. Doc. Ser. 557*, pp. 928-29.

delegates were Americans, only seven being native Californians. All seemingly were interested in the welfare of the province, although the question of state or territorial government almost resulted in a sharp division between the northern and the southern delegates.[58]

When General Riley announced the calling of a convention in his proclamation of June 3, he judiciously left the decision of establishing a state or territorial form of government to the delegates of the convention. The proclamation specifically stated that he extended a call "for a general convention for forming a state or a plan for territorial government." Sentiment, however, for state government seemed to be somewhat greater, especially in the northern areas. Organizational meetings of the delegates in various districts revealed that the feeling for statehood was much stronger. The delegates of San Francisco and San Jose, for example, expressed their determination to push solidly for a state government.[59]

It is somewhat incredible to observe how quickly and effortlessly the sentiment for state government in California was aroused. Previous to General Riley's proclamation, the Americans clamored for territorial government.[60] Once the proclamation was out and state government was mentioned as a possibility, almost to a man the supporters of territorial government switched to statehood. Without

---

[58] Browne, *Debates in the Convention,* pp. 7-10.
[59] *Alta California,* San Francisco, June 14, 1849.
[60] *Ibid.,* Jan. 4, 1849.

the motivating influence of loud-voiced orators or rousing editorials, the people of California instinctively reached for state government when they thought it a possibility.

At the convention, however, the opposition to state government was composed of a minority representing the southern districts in California where the large landholders did not wish to be taxed for the support of a state government. Some of these southern delegates even proposed dividing the territory of California into a state and a territory. Under the influence of Stephen C. Foster, however, this minority group finally agreed that, however loathsome state government might be, they would accept it rather than divide the province. Delegates of the convention then turned unhampered towards the work of establishing a state government and constitution.[61]

The administration of the government during the convention at Monterey continued its normal course under General Riley. Although he continued to make appointments to various offices in the municipal government, Riley refused to review cases of any of the lower courts, once the superior tribunal was established.[62] The convention, meanwhile, ran its normal course, and when the question of expenses of the convention delegates arose, it was decided to pay them out of the civil fund. General Riley had earlier made this suggestion,

[61] Browne, *Debates in the Convention*, p. 22.

[62] Halleck, Monterey, to J. W. Geary, San Francisco, Oct. 3, 1849, *U.S. Gov. Doc. Ser. 573*, p. 852.

which, seemingly, appealed to the convention.[63] Therefore, delegates were allowed sixteen dollars a day and sixteen dollars for every twenty miles traveled. Other officers at the convention were paid accordingly and ten thousand dollars were provided to

> . . . print and publish for the use of the state, one thousand copies in English and two hundred and fifty copies in Spanish of a stenographic report of the proceedings of the Convention.

On the last day of the meeting the convention adopted by unanimous vote the assigning of a retroactive ten thousand dollar annual salary to General Riley for his term as Governor of California. The Secretary of State, Captain H. W. Halleck, was given a salary of six thousand dollars a year.[64]

Once the constitution was framed, the convention provided for its ratification, assigning as election day Tuesday, November 13, 1849. The various printed copies of the constitution were distributed throughout the settlements in California along with a proclamation from General Riley which stated:

> The delegates of the people, assembled at Convention, have formed a Constitution, which is now presented for your ratification. The time and manner of voting on this Constitution, and of holding the first General Election, are clearly set forth in the schedule. The whole subject is therefore left to your unbiased and deliberate consideration. . .

---

[63] Browne, *Debates in the Convention,* pp. 163-4.
[64] *Ibid.,* pp. 94-6.

The people are now called upon to form a government for themselves, and to designate such officers as they desire to make and execute the laws. That their choice may be wisely made, and that the Government so organized may secure the permanent welfare and happiness of the people of the new State, is the sincere and earnest wish of the present executive, who, if the Constitution be ratified, will, with pleasure surrender his powers to whomsoever the people may designate as his successor.[65]

Two weeks before the election, on October 31, Governor Riley wrote to the Adjutant General in Washington, D.C. explaining the situation in California and attempting to justify the constitutional convention and the state government. He stated:

You will see by examining the schedule that it is contemplated to put the new government into operation on or soon after the fifteenth day of December next; and I shall then surrender my civil powers to whomsoever may be designated under the Constitution as the executive of the new State. Whatever may be the legal objections to putting into operation a State government previous to its being acknowledged or approved by Congress, these objections must yield to the obvious necessities of the case; for the powers of the existing government are too limited, and its organization too imperfect to provide for the wants of a country so peculiarly situated, and of a population with such unprecedented rapidity.[66]

The convention had optimistically declared that elections be held for lieutenant governor and for congressman on the same day the constitution was

[65] Proclamation, Riley, Monterey, Oct. 12, 1849, *U.S. Gov. Doc. Ser. 573*, pp. 861-2.

[66] Riley, Monterey, to R. Jones, Washington, Oct. 31, 1849, *U.S. Gov. Doc. Ser. 557*, pp. 810-11.

presented to the people for ratification.[67] Regarding the candidates for these offices, all of them ran independently except for three that were nominated by a nonpartisan meeting. This nonpartisan meeting, which was held at Monterey on November 1, extended to General Bennet Riley the nomination of governor, but the General declined to run. In his place the committee chose William A. Sherwood. F. J. Lippitt was selected for lieutenant governor and Edward Gilbert and James L. Ord for congressmen. Those who ran independently were Peter H. Burnett, John A. Sutter, William S. Stewart, and John W. Geary for governor; John McDougal, Richard Roman, John A. Frisbie, A. M. Winn and Pablo de la Guerra for lieutenant governor.[68]

The election was held as scheduled on November 13, which turned out to be a rather dreary, dismal day, and, as a result, a light vote was anticipated. The people, however, went to the polling places despite the rain, mud and slime. One voter commented:

> The Constitution for the State of California, which is now before the people for their ratification, is very popular and no doubt it will be adopted – for myself I cannot swallow the slavery prohibition and will vote with the opposition.[69]

[67] Constitution of California, R. Semple, Monterey, *U.S. Gov. Doc. Ser. 573,* p. 859.

[68] *Alta California,* San Francisco, Nov. 9, 1849; *Pacific News,* San Francisco, Nov. 15, 1849.

[69] Cornelius C. Cox, "The Cox Diary," p. 67.

Another voter noticed:

At Yorktown I voted at the election adopting the first Constitution of California. Ballots were received from natives, foreign-born, Indians, peon, everyone. No challenge is put in, no qualifications or questions were suggested or deemed requisite. It was a voting Saturnalia but nearly all on the affirmative side.[70]

The election returns clearly indicated the landslide victory for the State Constitution, 12,061 people voting for it, with only 811 against it. Peter H. Burnett was chosen as the first governor of California and John McDougal as the first lieutenant governor.[71]

The civil process was thus complete. The constitution had been established by a convention of elected delegates, and ratified by the people. At the same election a governor, lieutenant governor and various other officials were chosen. General Riley, therefore, on December 20, 1849, issued his last proclamation to the people of California in relinquishing control of the gubernatorial office:

A new executive having been elected and installed into office, in accordance with the provisions of the constitution of the State, the undersigned hereby resigns his power as governor of California. In thus dissolving his official connection with the people of this country, he would tender to them his most heartfelt thanks for the many kind attentions, and for the uniform support which they have given to the measures of his administration. The principal object

[70] Benjamin B. Harris, "Crumbs of '49," p. 48.
[71] Senator and Representatives elected . . . from California . . . , Mar. 18, 1850, *U.S. Gov. Doc. Ser. 581*, p. 14.

of all his wishes is now accomplished – the people have a
government of their own choice; one which, under the
favor of Divine Providence, will secure their own prosperity and happiness, and the permanence of the new
State.[72]

Thus ended the four and one half year tenure of
military government in California – a government
that was described by its critics as arbitrary and
dictatorial, and by its supporters as fair and expedient. And yet, despite all criticism, it served the
specific purpose of holding and governing enemy
occupied territory and, under various military
leaders who served as governors, it was efficiently
and conscientiously administered.

---

[72] Proclamation, Riley, Dec. 20, 1849, *U.S. Gov. Doc. Ser. 561*, p. 40.

Some Conclusions

Despite obvious benefits, government is, to many people, simply a necessary evil. Utterances to this effect clutter the pages of history and are directed against any government. Ralph Waldo Emerson's statement: "The less government we have, the better – the fewer laws, and the less confided powers," is fairly typical and represents a feeling shared by many people through history. Military government enjoys no immunity to the bitter generalizations. In point of fact, its arbitrary nature and wide jurisdictional powers make it particularly vulnerable to the criticism of the governed.

It is a matter of record that military government instituted by the United States prior to 1850 was consistently successful. Certainly this is patently evident in the record of its application in Louisiana, Florida, New Mexico and California, where it achieved its goal by supplying government, maintaining order, and occupying territory for the United States. In each area where it was instituted, however, military control became objectionable to the people, and some form of opposition to it developed. In Louisiana, Governor William C. C. Claiborne was looked upon with distrust, and by 1804 the inhabitants presented a

petition to both houses of Congress listing grievances resulting from military rule.

Governor Andrew Jackson's administration of
military government in Florida in 1821 was far
from peaceful. In New Mexico in 1846, Governor
Charles Bent, the appointee of General Kearny,
was murdered in an uprising of the inhabitants.
Yet despite the dissatisfaction with military government in Louisiana, Florida, and New Mexico,
there is no evidence that these governments were
particularly tyrannical or abusive. The chief
source of discontent, it seems, was the natural
odium felt against military authority by civilians.

In the occupation of California, Commodore
Sloat assumed a conciliatory attitude toward the
inhabitants but did very little in organizing the
military government during his short stay. The
more vigorous policy adopted by his successor,
Commodore Stockton, resulted in a serious uprising of the native Californians in September, 1846.
This, however, was the last organized opposition
to military rule by the native Californians. When
General Kearny succeeded to the governorship on
March 1, 1847, there were sufficient military
forces on hand to adequately control and govern
the province.

Both General Kearny and his successor, Colonel
Mason administered military government in California with a firm, but seemingly, fair hand. Their
appointment and close supervision of alcaldes char-
acterized their administrations. Colonel Mason,

who served the longest time as military governor, faced the most trying conditions. Increased desertions, after the gold discovery, crippled his forces. Opposition to military rule (now coming from American residents in California) mounted and became more threatening after the announcement of the Treaty of Guadalupe Hidalgo. Colonel Mason, however, managed to administer the military government as best he could until the arrival of his replacement General Riley.

The main opposition to military rule in California came from American residents, who not only disliked military authority but were greatly opposed to alcalde rule and justice. The Americans could neither understand nor accept the wide powers granted to this magistrate. When Congress, therefore, refused to provide civil government after California was officially annexed, the people increased their clamor for civil government. Mass meetings were held and the citizens seemed determined to have their way.

General Riley, who relieved Colonel Mason as governor on April 12, 1849, sensed the seriousness of the situation and determined to do something about it. First he professed to be a civil governor and then issued a proclamation calling for delegates to a convention to form "a state or plan for territorial government." The convention was held, a state constitution and government established, and on December 20, 1849, the military government relinquished its control to the newly-elected civil officials.

The people in California, despite decrying editorials in contemporary newspapers, were never seriously oppressed or mistreated by military rule. Indeed, the military authority embraced all levels of government, and many aspects of alcalde justice were strange. Nonetheless, few restrictions were placed on the individual citizen. The gold miners, for example, had virtually a free hand and were governed only by "local miner's law." In some respects, therefore, military government did not extend far enough, especially when the lawlessness of the Hounds in San Francisco is considered. It was the people themselves, virtually unaided by military forces, who put a stop to the nefarious activities of this group. Yet considering the meager forces available for its support, military government in California served the United States well. The province was occupied and held; lawlessness and disorder were kept to a minimum; and a self-supporting government was organized and maintained.

Bibliography and Index

Bibliography

I. GOVERNMENT PUBLICATIONS

American Insurance Company *v.* Cantor (1828), 1 Peters, 511.

American State Papers, Documents Legislative and Executive of the Congress of the United States. Vol. 1, Misc. Washington: Gales and Seaton, 1858.

Appendix, 1 Cal. Rep. 559.

Bean *v.* Beckwith (1873), 18 Wallace, 510.

Debates and Proceedings of the Congress of the United States. 8 Cong., 2 sess. (1803). Washington: Gales and Seaton, 1852.

Dooley *v.* United States (1901), 182 U.S., 222.

Dow *v.* Johnson (1879), 100 U.S., 166.

Downes *v.* Bidwell (1901), 182 U.S., 244.

Ex parte Milligan (1866), 4 Wallace, 2.

Mena *v.* Le Roy, 1 Cal. Rep. 216.

Recopilacion de Leyes de los Reynos de las Indias. Madrid: 1681.

Reglamento Para el Gobierno de la Provincia de Californias. Mexico: 1784.

Reynolds *v.* West, 1 Cal. Rep. 322.

U.S. Congress. Senate. Message of the President. 29 Cong., 2 sess., S. Doc. 1. Washington: 1846. Serial no. 493.

———. House. Occupation of Mexican Territory. 29 Cong., 2 sess., H. Doc. 19. Washington: 1846. Serial no. 499.

———. Senate. Gen. S. W. Kearny's Overland March. 30 Cong., 1 sess., S. Ex. Doc. 1. Washington: 1847. Serial no. 503.

———. Senate. Court-martial of J. C. Fremont. 30 Cong., 1 sess., S. Ex. Doc. 33. Washington: 1847. Serial no. 507.

U.S. Congress: Senate. California Claims. 30 Cong., 1 sess., S. Rep. 75. Washington: 1847. Serial no. 512.

————. House. Notes of a Military Reconnaissance. 30 Cong., 1 sess., H. Ex. Doc. 41. Washington: 1847. Serial no. 517.

————. House. The Mexican War. 30 Cong., 1 sess., H. Ex. Doc. 60. Washington: 1847. Serial no. 520.

————. House. New Mexico and California. 30 Cong., 1 sess., H. Ex. Doc. 70. Washington: 1847. Serial no. 521.

————. Senate. Report of the Secretary of the Navy. 30 Cong., 2 sess., S. Ex. Doc. 31. Washington: 1848. Serial no. 531.

————. House. Message from the President. 30 Cong., 2 sess., H. Ex. Doc. 1. Washington: 1848. Serial no. 537.

————. Senate. Operations in California. 31 Cong., 1 sess., S. Ex. Doc. 1. Washington: 1848. Serial no. 549.

————. Senate. Message of the President. 31 Cong., 1 sess., S. Ex. Doc. 18. Washington: 1849. Serial no. 557.

————. Senate. General B. Riley's Civil Correspondence. 31 Cong., 1 sess., S. Ex. Doc. 52. Washington: 1849. Serial no. 561.

————. House. California and New Mexico. 31 Cong., 1 sess., H. Ex. Doc. 17. Washington: 1849. Serial no. 573.

————. House. T. B. King's Report on California. 31 Cong., 1 sess., H. Ex. Doc. 59. Washington: 1850. Serial no. 577.

————. House. California Customs. 31 Cong., 1 sess., H. Ex. Doc. 72. Washington: 1850. Serial no. 578.

————. House. Memorial of Senators and Representatives Elect from California. 31 Cong., 1 sess., H. Misc. Doc. 44. Washington: 1850. Serial no. 581.

————. Senate. Fremont Claims. 34 Cong., 1 sess., S. Ex. Doc. 109. Washington: 1856. Serial no. 825.

————. Senate. Treaties, Conventions, International Acts and Agreements. 61 Cong., 2 sess., S. Doc. 357. Washington: 1910. Serial no. 5646.

II. MANUSCRIPT COLLECTIONS

Bancroft Library, University of California, Berkeley.
Archives of California, Unbound Documents.
Baldridge, William. The Days of 1846.
Bartlett, Washington. Statement . . . of a Pioneer of California.
Belden, Josiah. Statement of Historical Facts.
Bidwell, John. California, 1841-1848.
Bigler, Henry W. Diary of a Mormon in California.
Brown, Harvey S. Early Days in California.
Burnett, Peter Hardeman. Correspondence and Papers.
Chaffee, John A. Accounts and Miscellaneous Papers.
Chiles, J.B. A Visit to California in Early Times.
Crosby, E.O. Statements of Events in California.
Drinkwater, Sarah B. Family Correspondence.
Findla, James. Statement of a Few Events in the Early Days of California.
Folsom, Joseph L. Correspondence and Papers.
Foster, Stephen C. Alcalde of Los Angeles.
Letterbooks of John Montgomery, 1844-1848. Microcopy C-A 206, 2 reels.
Lieber, Francis. California Scrapbook.
Mason, Richard. Letters.
F. W. Morris Collection: California Military Government.
Pierce, Hiram D. Diary.
Riley, Bennet. Correspondence and Papers.
Royce, Josiah. Fremont Papers.
Ryland, Caius T. Connection with the History of California.
Sherman, Richard M. Recollections of California.
Sutter, John A. Personal Reminiscences.
Thurber, Albert K. Journal of Albert Thurber.
Walker, Joel P. Narrative of Adventures.
Weeks, William J. Reminiscences.

Wilson, Benjamin D.   Early Days in California.

Wilson, John.   Correspondence and Papers.

Huntington Library,   San Marino, California.

Cox, Cornelius.   The Cox Diary.

Davis, Benjamin.   Observations of Early Days in California and New Mexico.

Fort Sutter Papers.

Harris, Benjamin B.   Account of a Journey . . . to the Gold Mines.

————.   Crumbs of '49.

Leidesdorff, William A.   Papers.

Standage, Henry.   Journal of Henry Standage.

Stearns, Abel.   Stearns Collection.

Special Collections Library,   University of California at Los Angeles.

Gillespie, Archibald H.   Archibald H. Gillespie Collection.

Stevenson, Jonathan D.   J. D. Stevenson Collection.

National Archives,   Washington, D.C.

Pacific Squadron, Commodore J. S. Sloat's Cruise, Oct. 16, 1844 to Oct. 23, 1846. Navy Department, Letters Received by the Secretary of the Navy from Commanding Officers of Squadrons. Microfilm 89, roll no. 32.

Commodore R. F. Stockton's Correspondence, June 25, 1846-Feb. 18, 1848, Letters Received by the Secretary of the Navy from Commanding Officers of Squadrons. Microfilm 89, roll no. 33.

Letters Sent by the Military Governors and the Secretary of State of California, Mar. 1, 1847-Sept. 23, 1848. Microfilm 182, roll no. 1.

III.   NEWSPAPERS

The Californian,   Monterey, Aug. 15, 1846-Aug. 21, 1847.

Californian,   San Francisco, Aug. 28, 1847-Nov. 11, 1848.

The California Star,   San Francisco, Jan. 8-June 14, 1848.

The California Star and Californian. San Francisco, Nov. 18-
    Dec. 23, 1848.
Alta California. San Francisco, Jan. 4-Dec., 1849.
Pacific News, San Francisco, Aug. 25-Dec., 1849.
Placer Times, Sacramento, April 28-Dec., 1849.

IV. BOOKS, ARTICLES, THESES

Adams, E.D., "British Interest in California," American
    Historical Review, xiv (1919) 744-63.
"Administration of Justice in California," Littell's Living Age,
    xxv (1850) 354-56.
Ames, George W., ed. "A Doctor Comes to California: The
    Diary of John S. Griffin, Assistant Surgeon with Kearny's
    Dragoons, 1846-1847," California Historical Quarterly.
———. and Richard R. Stenberg, eds. "The Letters of
    Archibald Gillespie," California Historical Quarterly,
    xvii (1938) 123-40, 271-84, 325-50; xviii (1939) 217-
    28.
Bancroft, Hubert H. History of Arizona and New Mexico.
    San Francisco: The History Company, 1889.
———. History of California. Vols. v, vi. San Francisco:
    The History Company. 1886, 1887.
Barrows, David P., and Thomas N. Barrows. Government
    in California. New York: World Book Co., 1925.
Barry, Theodore A., and Benjamin A. Patten. Men and
    Memories of San Francisco. San Francisco: [n.p.] 1873.
Bassett, John S. The Life of Andrew Jackson. New York:
    The Macmillan Company, 1925.
Bayard, Samuel J. A Sketch of the Life of Commodore
    Robert F. Stockton. New York: Derby & Jackson, 1856.
Bender, A.B. "Frontier Defence in the Territory of New
    Mexico, 1846-1853." New Mexico Historical Review, ix
    (1934) 249-72.
Benton, Joseph A. California As She Was: As She Is: As
    She Is To Be. Sacramento: Placer Times Press, 1850.

Benton, Thomas A.   Thirty Years View; or A History of the Working of the American Government for Thirty Years, from 1820 to 1850. New York: D. Appleton & Co., 1856.

Bidwell, John.   In California before the Gold Rush. Los Angeles: Ritchie Press, 1848.

Birkhimer, William E.   Military Government and Martial Law. Washington: J. J. Chapman, 1892.

Blair, Charles A.   The Territorial Policy of the United States. Guthrie, Oklahoma: The State Capital Company, 1903.

Bloom, Lansing B. ed.   "A Group of Kearny Letters," New Mexico Historical Review, v (1930) 17-37.

Borthwick, J.D.   Three Years in California. Edinburgh: Wm. Blackwood & Sons, 1857.

Brevard, Caroline Mays.   A History of Florida. Deland, Florida: The Florida State Historical Society, 1924.

Brooks, B.S.   "Alcalde Grants in San Francisco," Pioneer Monthly (San Francisco, 1854), i, pp. 129-44.

Brown, James S.   Life of a Pioneer, Being the Autobiography of James S. Brown. Salt Lake City: Geo. Q. Cannon & Sons Co., 1900.

Browne, John Ross.   Reports of the Debates in the Convention of California on the Formation of the State Constitution in September and October, 1849. Washington: John C. Towers, 1850.

Bryant, Edwin.   What I Saw in California. New York: D. Appleton and Co., 1849.

Burnett, Peter H.   Recollections and Opinions of an Old Pioneer. New York: D. Appleton & Co., 1880.

Bynum, Lyndley.   "Laws for the Better Government of California, 1848," Pacific Historical Review, ii (1933) 279-91.

California: Its Past History: Its Present Condition: Its Future Prospects. London: M'Cowan and Co., 1850.

California: Its Present Condition and Future Prospects. Adelaide, Australia: Andrew Murray, 1850.

Camp, Charles L.   "Kit Carson in California," California Historical Quarterly, i (1922) 11.

Claiborne, W.C.C. Official Letterbooks of W. C. C. Claiborne, 1801-1816. Dunbar Rowland, ed. Jackson, Mississippi: State Department of Archives and History, 1917.

Clarke, Francis D. First Regiment of New York Volunteers, New York: G. S. Evans & Co., 1882.

Clarke, Dwight L. Stephen Watts Kearny. Norman: University of Oklahoma Press, 1961.

Cleland, Robert G. The Early Sentiment for Annexation of California. Austin: Texas State Historical Assn., [n.d.].

Colton, Walter. Three Years in California. New York: A. S. Barnes & Co., 1851.

Compiled Laws of New Mexico, 1897. Santa Fe, New Mexico: New Mexico Printing Co., 1897.

Cooke, Philip St. George. The Conquest of New Mexico and California. New York: G. P. Putnam's Sons, 1878.

Cowan, R.E. "Journal of John McHenry Hollingsworth, A Lieutenant in Stevenson's Regiment in California," California Historical Society Quarterly, XI (1923) 207-70.

Crosby, Elisha O. Memoirs of Elisha Oscar Crosby. Charles A. Barker, ed. San Marino, California: The Huntington Library, 1945.

Crotty, Homer D. "The California Constitutional Convention of 1849," Historical Society of Southern California Quarterly, XXXI (1949).

Cutts, James M. The Conquest of California and New Mexico. Philadelphia: Carey & Hart, 1850.

Davis, George B. A Treatise on the Military Law of the United States. London: John Wiley & Sons, 1909.

Ellison, Joseph. "California and the Nation," Southwest Historical Quarterly, XXX (1926-1927) 83-113.

———. "The Struggle for Civil Government in California, 1846-1850," Calif. Hist. Quarterly, X (1931) 220-44.

Ellison, William Henry. A Self Governing Dominion. Berkeley, California: University of California Press, 1950.

"Extracts From the Log of the U.S. Frigate Savannah Kept by Robert Carson Duvall," California Historical Quarterly, III (1924) 105-25.

Fairman, Charles. The Law of Martial Rule. Chicago: Callaghan and Co., 1930.

Field, Stephen J. Personal Reminiscences of Early Days in California. Printed for a few friends: 1893.

Fitch, George Hamlin, "How California Came into the Union," Century Magazine, XL (1890) 775-92.

Frankhauser, William C. A Financial History of California. Berkeley, California: University of California Press, 1913.

Fremont, John C. Memoirs of my Life. Chicago: Belford, Clarke & Co., 1887.

Frost, John. History of the State of California. New York: Derby and Miller, 1850.

Fuller, Hubert B. The Purchase of Florida. Cleveland: The Burrows Brothers Company, 1906.

Gayarre, Charles. History of Louisiana: the American Domination. New Orleans: Armand Hawkins, 1885.

Giffen, Guy J. California Expedition: Stevenson's Regiment. Oakland, California: Biobooks, 1951.

————, and Helen Giffen, "Tracing Fremont's Route with The California Battalion," Historical Society of Southern California Quarterly, XXII (1940).

Gill, William. California Letters. New York: Downs Printing Co., 1922.

Goodwin, Cardinal. John Charles Fremont. Palo Alto, California: Stanford University Press, 1930.

————. The Establishment of State Government in California. 1846-1850. New York: The Macmillan Co., 1914.

Grivas, Theodore. "General Stephen Watts Kearny and the Army of the West," Unpublished Master's Thesis, University of Southern California, 1953.

Hall, Frederick. History of San Jose and Surroundings. San Francisco: A. L. Bancroft & Co., 1871.

Halleck, H.W. International Law. New York: B. Van Nostrand, 1861.

Halleck, J. [sic], and W. E. P. Hartnell. Translation and Digest of Such Portions of the Mexican Laws of March 20 and May 23, 1837 as are Supposed to be Still in Force

and Adopted to the Present Condition of California. San
Francisco: Alta California, 1849.

Hittell, Theodore H.   History of California. San Francisco:
N. J. Stone & Company, 1898. Vol. II.

Hughes, John T.   Doniphan's Expedition. Cincinnati: O. P.
James, 1847.

Hunt, Rockwell D.   The Genesis of California's First Constitution. Baltimore: Johns Hopkins University Press,
1895.

————.   The Legal Status of California, 1846-49. Philadelphia: American Academy of Political and Social Science,
1899.

James, Marquis.   The Life of Andrew Jackson. Indianapolis:
Bobbs-Merrill Company, 1938.

Johnston, Abraham R., Marcellus B. Edwards, and Philip G.
Ferguson.   Marching with the Army of the West, 1846-
1848. Ralph P. Bieber, ed. Southwest Historical Series,
IV. Glendale, California: The Arthur H. Clark Co., 1936.

Kearny, Thomas,   "The Mexican War and the Conquest of
California," California Historical Quarterly, III (1929).

Kelly, George, ed.   "Coming of the Kearny Expedition Establishing U.S. Authority," Arizona Historical Rev., 33-49.

Kelsey, Rayner W.   The United States Consulate in California. Berkeley: University of California Press, 1910.

Kip, Leonard.   California Sketches with Recollections of the
Gold Mines. Albany, New York: Erastus H. Pease & Co.,
1850.

Laws for the Better Government of California, the Preserva-
tion of Order, and the Protection of the Rights of the
Inhabitants, During the Military Occupation of the
Country by the Forces of the United States.   By Author-
ity of R. B. Mason, Col. 1st U.S. Drags. & Governor.
San Francisco: Published by S. Brannan, 1848.

Laws of the Town of San Francisco, 1847. San Marino, California: Published by the Friends of the Huntington
Library, 1947.

Lippitt, Francis J. Reminiscences. Providence, Rhode Island: Preston & Rounds Co., 1902.

Lorimer, James. The Institutes of the Law of Nations. Edinburgh: William Blackwood and Sons, 1884.

M'Collum, William. California As I Saw It. Buffalo, New York: George H. Derby & Co., 1850.

Martin, Francois X. The History of Louisiana. New Orleans: Lyman and Beardslee, 1828-29.

Martin, Sidney W. Florida during the Territorial Days. Athens, Georgia: University of Georgia Press, 1944.

Montgomery, John B. A Proclamation to the Inhabitants of Northern District of California. San Francisco: S. Brannan, 1846.

Moses, Bernard. The Establishment of Municipal Government in San Francisco. Baltimore: The Johns Hopkins Press, 1889.

Polk, James K. The Diary of James K. Polk During His Presidency, 1845-1849. Milo M. Quaife, ed. Chicago: A. C. McClurg & Co., 1910.

Poole, Edward L. A Thousand and One Nights. New York: P. F. Collier & Sons Corp., 1937.

Porter, V.M. "General Stephen W. Kearny and the Conquest of California," Annual Publication Historical Society of Southern California, VIII (1911).

Proceedings of the Town Council of San Francisco. San Francisco: Alta California, 1850.

Revere, Joseph W. A Tour of Duty. Joseph N. Balestiar, ed. New York: C. S. Francis & Co., 1949.

———. Keel and Saddle. Boston: James R. Osgood and Company, 1872.

———. Naval Duty in California. Oakland, California: Biobooks, 1947.

Robertson, James A. Louisiana Under the Rule of Spain, France and the United States. Cleveland: The Arthur H. Clark Co., 1911.

Robertson, James R.   "From Alcalde to Mayor; A History of
    the Change from Mexican to the American Institutions
    of California." Berkeley, California: Unpublished Doc-
    toral Dissertation, University of California, 1908.
Robinson, Alfred.   Life in California. New York: Wiley and
    Putnam, 1846.
Robinson, W.W.   Lawyers of Los Angeles. Los Angeles Bar
    Association, 1959.
Root, Riley.   Journal of Travels from St. Joseph to Oregon,
    with Observations of that Country with a Description of
    California, its Agricultural Interests and a Full Descrip-
    tion of its Gold Mines. Galesburg, Illinois: Gazetteer and
    Intelligencer Prints, 1850.
Royce, C.C.   John Bidwell, Pioneer, Statesman, Philan-
    thropist. Chico, California: 1906.
Royce, Josiah.   California from the Conquest in 1846 to the
    Second Vigilance Committee in San Francisco. Boston:
    Houghton Mifflin & Co., 1886.
————,   "Light on the Seizure of California," The Century
    Magazine XL (1890), 792-94.
Ryan, William Redmond.   Personal Adventures. London:
    William Shoberl, 1850.
Schoonover, T.J.   Life and Times of Gen. John A. Sutter.
    Sacramento: Bullock Corp., 1907.
Sherman, Edwin A.   The Life of the Late Rear Admiral John
    D. Sloat. Oakland, California: Carruth & Carruth,
    Printers, 1902.
Sherman, William T.   Home Letters of General Sherman.
    M. A. Dewolf Howe, ed. New York: Charles Scribner's
    Sons, 1909.
————.   Memoirs of General W. T. Sherman.   New York:
    Charles L. Webster & Co., 1891.
Shinn, Charles H.   Mining Camps; A Study in American
    Frontier Government. New York: Scribner's, 1885.
————,   "Some California Documents," Magazine of Amer-
    ican History, XXV (1891) 394-401.

Soule, Frank, John H. Gihon and James Nisbet.   The Annals
    of San Francisco. New York: D. Appleton & Co., 1854.

Streeter, William.   "Recollection of Historical Events in Cal-
    ifornia, 1843-1878," William H. Ellison, ed. California
    Historical Quarterly, xviii (1939) 64, 157, 254.

Swasey, W.F.   The Early Days and Men of California. Oak-
    land, California: Pacific Press Publishing Company, 1891.

Sweeny, Thomas W.   Military Occupation of California,
    1849-53. New York: Military Service Institution, 1905.

Taylor, Bayard.   Eldorado; or Adventures in the Path of
    Empire. New York: George Putnam & Co., 1850.

Thomas, David Y.   A History of Military Government in
    Newly Acquired Territory of the United States. New
    York: Columbia University Press, 1904.

Tower, Grace E.   "Sentiment in California for American
    Government and Admission into the Union." Los An-
    geles: Unpublished Master's Thesis, University of South-
    ern California, 1924.

Tuthill, Franklin.   The History of California. San Francisco:
    H. H. Bancroft, 1866.

Twitchell, Ralph E.   The Leading Facts of New Mexican
    History. Cedar Rapids, Iowa: The Torch Press, 1912.

Tyson, James L.   Diary of a Physician in California. New
    York: D. Appleton & Company, 1850.

Van Sicklen, Helen Putnam.   "The Life and Times of Gen-
    eral M. G. Vallejo," Quarterly of the Society of Califor-
    nia Pioneers, ix (1932) 143-60.

Walpole, Frederick.   Four Years in the Pacific in Her
    Majesty's Ship "Collingwood." London: Richard Bentley,
    1849.

Warren, Viola Lockhart.   "Dr. John S. Griffin's Mail, 1846-
    53," California Historical Quarterly, xxxiii (1954) 97.

[White, William F.]   A Picture of Pioneer Times in Califor-
    nia, by William Grey [pseud.]. San Francisco: W. M.
    Hinton, 1881.

Whiting, William.   Military Government of Hostile Terri-
    tory in Time of War. Boston: J. L. Shorey, 1864.

Wilkes, Charles. Western America, including California and Oregon, with maps . . . of the Sacramento Valley. Philadelphia: Lea & Blanchard, 1849.

———. Narrative of the United States Exploring Expedition During the Years 1838-1842. Philadelphia: C. Sherman, 1844.

Willey, Rev. Samuel Hippins. "Recollections of General Halleck as Secretary of State in Monterey, 1847-9," Overland Monthly, IX (1872) 9-11.

———. Thirty Years in California. San Francisco: A. L. Bancroft, 1879.

———. The Transition Period of California from a Province of Mexico in 1846 to a State of the American Union in 1850. San Francisco: The Whitaker and Ray Company, 1901.

Williams, Mary Floyd. History of the San Francisco Committee of Vigilance of 1851. Berkeley, California: University of California Press, 1921.

———. "Mission, Presidio and Pueblo," California Historical Quarterly, I (1922) 23-35.

Wise, Henry Augustus. Los Gringos. New York: Baker and Scribner, 1849.

Wright, Flora Alice. "Richard Barnes Mason, Governor of California." Berkeley: Unpublished Master's Thesis, University of California, 1919.

Index

ADAMS, John Q: 18
Adams-Onis Treaty: 29
Alabama: 27
Alcalde: appointee in Florida, 30; some offices elected, 87; districts, 88; Stockton proclaims election of, 88; incumbents to stay, 88; Stockton appointments, 107; appointments in Sonoma, 107; authority, 109; justice, 111; criminal justice, 112; jurisdiction, 112; opposition by military authority, 116; in mining districts, 134; origin, 151; various types, 151; elected, 153; qualifications for office, 155; appointive procedures, 156; jurisdiction, 157; powers, 159; courts defined, 159-61; Court of First Instance, 161; legislative duties, 163; executive duties, 164; pueblo lands, 164; elections, 170; contemporary description of, 171; introduction of juries, 173, 174; close supervision of, 176; Mason appointments, 177; effect of Gold Rush, 178; in mining areas, 178; typical fines, 179; courts over crowded, 181; unusual decisions, 182-84; attacks on by press, 189-90; lynch law, 179; system criticized, 197-98
Almond, William B: 181
Alvarado, Juan Bautista: 95
Ambrister, Robert: 28

Arbuthnot, Alexander: 28
Arguello, Santiago: 95, 98
Army of the West: 32, 47
Aury, Luis: 29
Ayuntamiento: 113, 162

BANCROFT, George: 42-43
Bancroft Library: 11
Bandini, Juan: 95
Bartlett, Washington: 57, 89, 174-75
Bates, Frank: 183-84
Battle of Dominguez Ranch: 58
Battle of San Pasqual: 60
Bear Flag Revolt: 48
Bell, Alexander: 88
Bellemy, George W: 100
Bent, Charles: 37, 38
Benton, Thomas H: 74, 204-206
Biddle, James: 104
Blackberry, William: 183
Boggs, Lilburn: 107
Brackenridge, Henry M: 31
Brackett, John E: 14
Brannon, Sam: 120
Brown, Hedy C: 115
Brown, John: 57
Bryant, Edwin: 107
Buchanan, James A: 126, 203
Burnett, Peter H: elected first governor, 79, 148, 218-19; chief justice, 146; portrait, 168; views on independent government, 197
Burton, Victor: 176